The OXFORD Children's A to Z of Technology

Robin Kerrod

OXFORD UNIVERSITY PRESS

Oxford University Press, Walton Street, Oxford, OX2 6DP

Oxford New York Athens Auckland Bangkok Bogotá
Bombay Buenos Aires Calcutta Cape Town Dar es
Salaam Delhi Florence Hong Kong Istanbul Karachi
Kuala Lumpur Madras Madrid Melbourne Mexico City
Nairobi Paris Singapore Taipei Tokyo Toronto

and associated companies in
Berlin Ibadan

Oxford is a trade mark of Oxford University Press

© Robin Kerrod 1996

First published in 1996
10 9 8 7 6 5 4 3 2 1

ISBN 019 910359 3 (hardback)
ISBN 019 910088 8 (paperback)

A CIP catalogue record for this book is available
from the British Library

Printed in Italy by G. Canale & C. S.p.A.
Borgaro T.se - TURIN

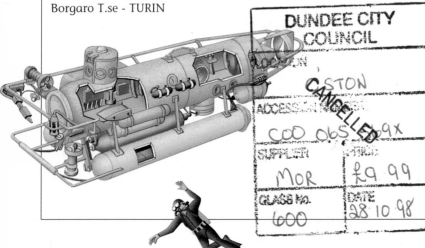

Acknowledgements

Design and art direction: Vivienne Gordon
Picture research: Charlotte Lippmann

Abbreviations: t = top; b = bottom; l = left; r = right;
c = centre; back = background

Photographs

The publishers would like to thank the
following for permission to reproduce the
following photographs:

British Airways: 4c, 58/59c;
BT: 14 heading panel, 15t;
Mary Evans Picture Library: 14bc;
French Railways: 56t;
Robert Harding Picture Library: l9br/J.H.C. Wilson,
24tl, 41cl, 44b;
The Image Bank: 5b/Harald Sund, 9tr/Eric
Schweikardt, 17br, 18bl, 22/23t/Romilly Lockyer,
31br/P&G Bowater, 34 heading panel, 35t/Lars
Ternblad, 40b/Lou Jones, 43b/Dana Coffey,
48b/Guido Alberto Rossi, 49r/Obremski, 52/53t
Antonio Rosario, 55t/Ronald R. Johnson, 59t/Steve
Dunwell;
Lifefile: 25c, 57b/Emma Lee, 33c Nigel Sitwell;
London Aerial Photo Library: 58 back;
Oxford Scientific Films: 53b/Norbert Wu;
Q.A. Photos/Eurotunnel: 60t;
Raleigh: 7b;
Science Photo Library: 6/7bc/Paul Shambroom,
8/9b/NASA, 11tr/Steve Percival, 13bl/David Parker,
14 back/NASA, 17tl/James King-Holmes,
20/21c/Manfred Kage, 21tl/Charles Lightdale,
27t/JohnMead, 29c/Alexander Isiaras, 36b/Michael
W. Davidson, 39tr/Malcolm Fielding, 41 back /
Department of Clinical Radiology, Salisbury District
Hospital, 45b/David Parker, 46t/Francois Gohier, 50
(heading panel), back/ NASA, 51c, b/NASA,
61b/Geoff Tompkinson, 63tl/B1air Seitz;
Martin Soukias: 30tl, 64l;
Tony Stone Images: 13tl/Douglas/Struthers,
14br/Jon Riley, 28b/Poulides/Thatcher, 54t/Jon Gray,
55br/Aaron Jones-Studios;
The Telegraph Colour Library: 23br/I. Murphy,
31t/Colorific!/John Moss, 43t/M. Lynch, 62b;
Mark Wagner: 5t, 26bl

Illustrations and diagrams

Gecko Ltd: 38;
John Haslam: front cover tl and r, back cover r and cb,
1tl, 2c and cr, 3cl, c and cr (cog wheels), 4t and c,
10t, 12, 13r, 16, 18t, 19t, 20t, 22l, 30r, 32, 33b, 34b,
36t, 37r, 39tl and c, 40t, 42br, 47t, 48t and c, 52b,
57t, 61t, 64c;
Nick Hawken: front cover cl;
Ian Howatson: 1tr, 2b, 3tc and tr, 8l, 20b, 23t, 24b,
25r, 37tc, 41br, 42cl, 44t, 45t, 51t, 53cr, 54b, 56c,
60c, 62c;
Joe Lawrence: front cover bl, back cover tl, 1b, 3cr
(wheels) and b, 6bl, 7t, 10b, 11b, 15b, 17b, 27bl
and br, 28c, 29t and cl, 35b, 42 back, 45c, 47b, 49c,
59cr, 63r;
Martin Woodward: 39b

Dear Reader

Technology puts science to work for us. You can find technology all around you – in the materials you use, in the machines you work, and in all the different products that you buy. Technology affects every part of your life, from the moment when the alarm clock wakes you up in the morning to the time when you switch off your bedside light at night.

New technologies have made this age a very exciting one to live in. This is an age of automation and atom-smashers, e-mail and endoscopes, faxes and floppy disks, hydrofoils and hovercraft, modems and multimedia, pacemakers and polymers, robots and rocket motors, CDs, CFCs, LCDs, TGVs and VDUs.

If you are not quite sure what these marvels of modern technology are, then look inside this book to find out. But this is not just a book about basic everyday technologies; it tells you about the more advanced ones too. So on your way from **abacus** to **zip fastener**, you can also find out about ball-bearings and gears, dams and bridges, nuts and bolts, radio telescopes and refrigerators, tools and telephones, watches, wheels and winches and over 350 other terms.

This book will be a useful companion to you as you make your way through today's complex world. Use it as a dictionary or browse through it in your spare time, but be warned: once you have opened its pages, you will find it hard to put this book down!

Robin Kerrod

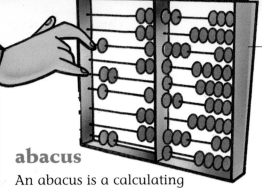

abacus

An abacus is a calculating machine that has been used for thousands of years. It has beads or rings which you move along wires inside a frame. It is still used in Russia, China and other Far Eastern countries.

You can count and do sums on an abacus by sliding beads along wires.

aeroplane

An aeroplane, or plane for short, is the commonest kind of aircraft. It has wings that support it in the air. It also has a tail, which helps it to fly straight. Planes have either jet engines or engines that turn **propellers**. Jet planes are the fastest aeroplanes. Some can travel at speeds of more than 3000 kilometres (km) per hour. See also **jet**, **jet engine**, **transport**.

This passenger plane is a Boeing 777. It can carry up to about 280 passengers, and cruises at a speed of about 890 kilometres (km) per hour.

acid rain

Acid rain is a kind of **pollution**. It is caused by gases from factory chimneys and car exhausts. The gases combine with water droplets in the air to form acid. The acid falls to the ground in rain.

Acid rain attacks the stonework of buildings, damages trees and harms water and the plants and animals that live in it.

adhesive

An adhesive is a sticky solution or mixture. You use it to join two surfaces together. Glue is an adhesive that has been used for hundreds of years. Modern adhesives include rubber solutions and plastic mixtures.

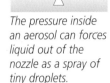

nozzle

fine spray

button

liquid that turns to spray

gas under pressure

The pressure inside an aerosol can forces liquid out of the nozzle as a spray of tiny droplets.

aerosol can

An aerosol can sprays out liquid as a fine mist. The liquid is kept inside the can under pressure. When you press a button, the liquid spurts out as a fine spray. Aerosol cans may contain liquids such as hair lacquer, furniture polish, paint and **pesticides**.

air conditioning

Air conditioning means controlling the state, or condition, of the air inside a room or building. An air conditioner can warm or cool the air, no matter what the temperature is like outside. It can also change the humidity (the amount of moisture in the air). Air conditioning can remove dirt and bad smells from the air.

aircraft

See **transport**.

aerial

An aerial sends out or receives radio signals. It is used in **communications**. An aerial may be a wire, a rod or a metal dish. It is sometimes called an antenna.
See also **radio**.

air resistance

When something moves through the air, the air pushes against it and tries to hold it back. This force is called air resistance. Aircraft, cars and other vehicles are often **streamlined** to reduce air resistance.
See also **drag**.

airship

An airship is a powered aircraft that stays up in the air because it is lighter than air. Airships were the first aircraft to carry passengers over long distances, in the early 1900s. Only a few are flying today.

An airship is really a very large balloon filled with a light gas. It is driven through the air by **propellers** that are powered by engines.

Modern airships like this one are filled with helium gas. Early ones were filled with hydrogen gas, which can easily catch fire.

alloy

An alloy is a mixture of two or more metals. The silver-coloured coins in your pocket are made from an alloy of copper and nickel, called cupronickel. Copper-coloured coins are made from an alloy of copper, tin and a little zinc. It is called bronze. Most cutlery is made of stainless steel. Stainless steel is a mixture of three main metals – iron, chromium and nickel.

Our most widely used metal, ordinary steel, is an alloy. It contains iron and tiny amounts of a non-metal called carbon.
See also **steel-making.**

alternative energy

Alternative energy is energy that we can produce without burning **fossil fuels.** Alternative energy includes geothermal power, hydroelectric power, solar power and wind and wave power.

Alternative energy has several advantages. Its sources, such as wind and energy from the Sun, will never run out. Also, they do not cause pollution like fossil fuels. There are not enough alternative energy schemes yet to supply the energy needs of all the world.
See also **geothermal power, hydroelectric power, solar power, wave power, wind power.**

Wind 'farms' use the power of the wind to supply alternative energy. This wind farm is at Altamont Pass in California, USA.

alternator

An alternator is a kind of **generator**.

antenna

See **aerial**.

aqueduct

An aqueduct is built to carry water. It may be a tunnel, a pipeline or an open channel.

arch

An arch is a curved structure that is used in building. Arches are strong because of their shape. They are widely used in building bridges and dams.

assembly line

See **making and manufacturing**.

atomic bomb

See **nuclear weapon**.

atom-smasher

An atom-smasher is a machine that breaks up atoms. (An atom is the smallest possible part of any substance.) Its correct name is particle accelerator. Atom-smashers use huge amounts of electricity and magnetism to speed up, or accelerate, beams of very tiny atomic parts called particles. Then they smash the atoms with these beams.

automation

See **making and manufacturing**.

Railway wagons use axles like this. The wheels have overlapping rims, called flanges, to keep them on the rails.

bearing

axle

wheel

axle

An axle is a rod, or shaft, that carries one or more wheels. The wheels spin around on the axle. Usually, a wheel is fitted onto an axle with a **bearing**. The bearing helps the wheel to turn more easily.

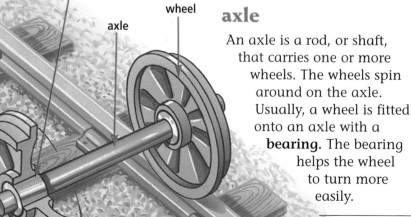

rail

ball-bearing

See **bearing**.

balloon

A balloon is a simple kind of aircraft. It consists of a large bag that is filled with gas. The gas needs to be lighter than air to make the balloon rise up into the air. Some balloons use hot air as the lifting gas, but others use helium gas.

ballpoint pen

A ballpoint pen uses a tiny moving ball to spread ink. When you write with a ballpoint, the ball rolls across the paper. As it rolls, it spreads the ink from a thin tube inside the pen.

bar code

Most goods that are sold in shops have a bar code. It is a pattern of black and white stripes, with a row of numbers below the stripes. The bar code on an object carries coded information about what kind of product it is. Many shops have a machine that 'reads' bar codes. It sends information about a product to a computer, which tells salespeople the product's price and how many of it are in stock.

At many supermarket tills, a laser beam 'reads' the bar codes as goods are passed over a window.

battery

A battery produces electricity. It is used to make things like torches and radios work. The battery in a car helps to start the engine and keep it running. The commonest battery is the dry battery, or dry cell. It has a zinc case filled with a chemical paste. There is a carbon rod in the middle of the battery. All these materials react together to produce electricity. The batteries in cars contain lead plates that are dipped in acid.

beam

A beam is a straight piece of wood, metal or other material. It is designed to carry a load. Metal beams called girders are used in many buildings, including bridges and skyscrapers.

bearing

A bearing is used in a machine which has moving parts. Bearings do two main things. They support the moving parts. They also reduce the **friction** (rubbing) between the moving and fixed parts. Bearings are found, for example, in the hub (centre) of bicycle wheels. They support the wheel **axle** and let it turn freely in the hub.

The inside of a dry battery, or dry cell. Chemicals are sealed inside the zinc case.

cap (terminal)

plastic cover

chemical paste

zinc case

chemicals

carbon rod

base (terminal)

bicycle

A bicycle, or bike for short, has two wheels that are held in a frame. When you pedal, a system of toothed **cog wheels** and a chain make the back wheel turn and move you forwards. You steer the bike by moving the handlebars, which turn the front wheel. Most bikes have several gears, which let you change your speed. The bike is one of the most popular forms of transport in the world.

This mountain bike has many gears to help the rider climb steep slopes.

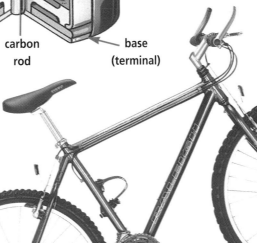

binoculars

You look through a pair of binoculars to see distant objects more clearly. Binoculars are a type of double telescope to use with both eyes. They have pieces of glass called lenses. The lenses produce bigger images (pictures) of distant objects.

bionics

Bionics is a short name for biological electronics. Bionic engineers develop electronic systems that work like real systems in living things. Some artificial limbs are bionic. They work by using tiny electrical currents that are produced by muscles in the human body.

biotechnology

In biotechnology, scientists make products by using tiny living things called organisms. The organisms are mostly so tiny that you need a microscope to see them. That is why they are called micro-organisms. Biotechnologists use micro-organisms such as bacteria and moulds, for example, to make some kinds of drugs.
See also **genetic engineering.**

bit

A bit is the smallest piece of information that a computer can handle. Bit is short for binary digit. There are just two binary digits, 0 and 1. Computers handle information in groups of bits called bytes.

valve

loading skip

In a blast furnace, iron forms when a mixture of iron ore, coke and limestone is heated to a temperature of about 1500 degrees Celsius (°C).

air blasted in here

blast furnace

A blast furnace uses heat to help separate, or extract, metals from their **ores**. This process is called smelting. Air is blasted into the furnace to make the fuel inside it burn fiercely. Iron is the most important metal produced in blast furnaces.

slag (waste)   iron

hot air in

furnace lining

block and tackle

A block and tackle is a group of **pulleys.** It is used to lift heavy loads. Garage mechanics may use a block and tackle to lift the engine out of a car.

blueprint

See **plans.**

bolt

A bolt is a metal pin with a head at one end and a screw thread at the other. It is used with a nut to join together pieces of metal and other materials. A nut has a matching thread, and screws onto the bolt. You use a spanner to turn the bolt head and nut.

brake

A brake slows down or stops moving vehicles or other moving things. Many brakes work by **friction** (rubbing). They are forced against moving parts, and the rubbing action causes the parts to slow down. Cars have this kind of brake on all four wheels. The space shuttle uses rockets to brake before it returns to Earth and a parachute after it has landed.

waste gases out

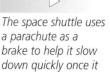

The space shuttle uses a parachute as a brake to help it slow down quickly once it has landed.

brazing

Brazing is a method of joining metal parts using a metal called brass. The brass is heated until it becomes liquid, and it is then dripped onto the parts to be joined. When the brass cools, it hardens and forms a strong joint. Bicycle frames are made by brazing.

brick

Bricks have been one of the most common building materials for thousands of years. They are very hard blocks of clay that have been strongly heated, or fired, inside a special oven called a kiln. In house-building, a kind of concrete called mortar is placed between layers of bricks to bond them strongly together. In some countries with a hot climate, bricks may be made from mud and dried in the sun.
See also **materials.**

bridge

A bridge carries a road or railway across a river, a valley or another obstacle. The simplest bridge is a **beam** that is supported at each end by pillars. Beam bridges cannot stretch across wide gaps, so other kinds must be used, such as arch bridges and suspension bridges. In a suspension bridge, the road hangs from wire cables.

Cables help to strengthen the middle part of this long beam bridge at St Petersburg in Florida, USA.

broadcasting

See **communications.**

bulldozer

A bulldozer is a powerful machine for moving earth. It has a steel blade at the front to move rocks, soil, tree stumps and other obstacles.

bullet train

A bullet train is a high-speed train that is shaped rather like a bullet. Bullet trains are **streamlined** so that they can travel faster.

bus

A bus is a vehicle that carries passengers over short distances. Bus is short for omnibus. A bus that is built to travel over quite long distances is usually called a coach.
See also **transport.**

CAD

See **design**.

calculator

You use a calculator to do sums. An **abacus** is a simple calculator. Calculating machines with gears were used in the 1600s. Most calculators today are electronic. They are simple computers.

camcorder

A camcorder is a combined video camera and videocassette recorder. The latest ones are small, light and easy to use. People use them to make their own video recordings. See also **videocassette recorder**.

camera

You use a camera to take photographs. A simple camera is a lightproof box. It has a piece of film at one end and a hole, called the aperture, at the other. When you press a button, a blind, or shutter, in front of the aperture opens briefly to let in the light. A lens focuses the light onto the film, which records an image (picture).

In many cameras, you can change the speed of the shutter and the size of the aperture. The lens can be moved in and out to focus on objects at different distances. See also **cine camera**.

A look inside a compact camera. The speed of the shutter and the aperture size are set automatically to take the best picture.

canal

A canal is an artificial waterway. Most canals are built to carry boats and ships. Some carry water for irrigation (watering farmland) and water supplies to towns. Two famous canals are the Suez Canal in Egypt and the Panama Canal in Central America. They carry ocean-going ships.

A cassette tape used for recording sound. Tapes like this are played in personal stereos, for example.

canning

See **food technology**.

car

See **motor car**.

cassette

A cassette is a sealed case that contains a reel of film or tape. Audio (sound) and video tapes come in cassettes that you simply slot into recording machines. See also **videocassette recorder**.

reels · magnetic tape · protective case · shutter release button · auto focus window · viewfinder · flashli · film cassette · film · aperture · lens · batter

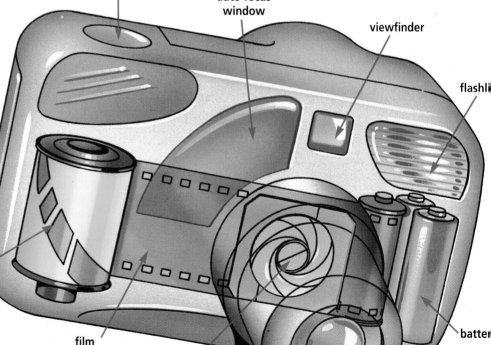

casting

Casting is a method of shaping objects by pouring a hot liquid into a mould. The main part of a car engine is made by pouring hot liquid iron into a shaped mould. When the iron cools and turns solid, it has the same shape as the mould.

A casting is the shaped metal object that is made by the method of casting.
See also **moulding.**

catalytic converter

A catalytic converter can be fitted to the exhaust pipe of a car. It contains a chemical called a catalyst. The catalyst changes, or converts, harmful gases from the car engine into harmless ones.
See also **motor car.**

cathode-ray tube

A cathode-ray tube (CRT) changes electrical signals into pictures. It forms the main part of a television set. In a CRT, beams of tiny particles, called electrons, are fired at a screen and make it glow. The beams build up a picture as they travel quickly backwards and forwards across the screen in a series of lines.
See also **television.**

CD

A CD, or compact disc, is a small, round piece of plastic and metal. It is used to record music and other sounds. Sound signals are recorded on a CD in code, in a pattern of tiny pits (sunken areas). When you play the disc, a **laser** beam inside the CD player reads the coded pattern. The code is changed back into sound signals, which then go to **loudspeakers.**

Other CDs can record words, photographs and movies as well as sound.
See also **CD-ROM.**

This compact disc is used to record music. It measures just 12 centimetres (cm) across.

Inside the cathode-ray tube, an electron gun fires beams of electrons at the screen. The focusing coil bends the beams so that they move backwards and forwards across the screen.

CD-ROM

A CD-ROM is a compact disc that stores many different kinds of information. This information may be words, photographs, video, pictures or sound. You can play back the disc through a computer or a television set. A single CD-ROM can hold all the words and pictures of a large encyclopedia.
See also **multimedia.**

cement

Cement is a grey powder. It is made by roasting a mixture of iron ore, limestone and clay in a **kiln.** Cement is mixed with sand, gravel and water to make concrete, one of our most useful building materials.
See also **materials.**

electron gun

electron beams

cathode-ray tube

focusing coil

mask

electron beams

coating on back of screen

screen

central heating

Central heating is a heating system for buildings. The heat is produced in one place and then distributed to the various rooms. Oil or gas is usually burned to heat up water in a boiler. The hot water is then pumped through pipes to the rooms. There, it passes through tubes inside the radiators, which give out the heat.

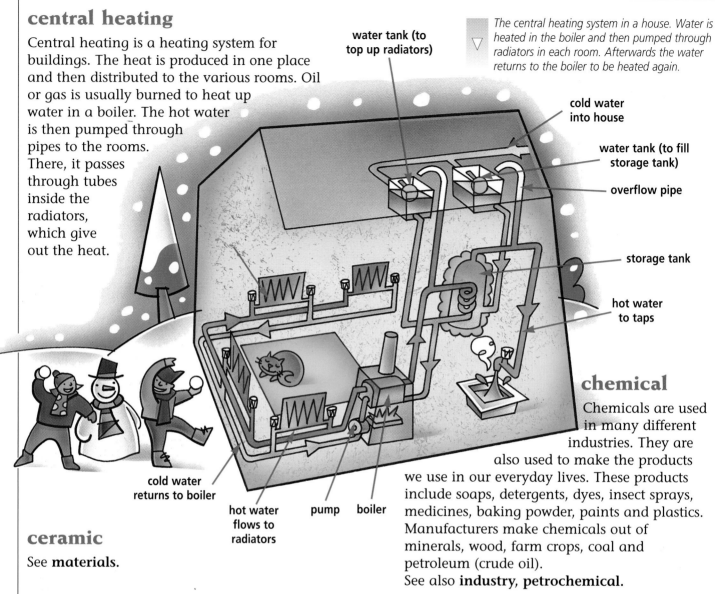

The central heating system in a house. Water is heated in the boiler and then pumped through radiators in each room. Afterwards the water returns to the boiler to be heated again.

water tank (to top up radiators)

cold water into house

water tank (to fill storage tank)

overflow pipe

storage tank

hot water to taps

cold water returns to boiler

hot water flows to radiators

pump

boiler

ceramic

See **materials**.

CFC

CFCs are liquid mixtures that contain the **chemicals** chlorine, fluorine and carbon. Their full name is chlorofluorocarbons. They were once widely used in refrigerators and aerosol spray cans, and to make foam products. They are used less now because scientists think that they can cause **pollution**.

chain

A chain is a series of rings that are joined together. These rings, or links, are usually made of metal. Chains are used in machines to move, or transfer, power from one place to another. In a bicycle, a chain transfers pedal power to the back wheel.

chemical

Chemicals are used in many different industries. They are also used to make the products we use in our everyday lives. These products include soaps, detergents, dyes, insect sprays, medicines, baking powder, paints and plastics. Manufacturers make chemicals out of minerals, wood, farm crops, coal and petroleum (crude oil).
See also **industry, petrochemical**.

chisel

See **tool**.

cine camera

People use a cine camera to make movies, or motion pictures. It takes a series of pictures quickly, one after the other. The camera has a shutter, a lens and a film like an ordinary camera. A motor moves the film through the camera. The film stops for a tiny part of a second while each picture is taken.
See also **camera, movie**.

cinema

See **movie**.

clock

A clock measures time. For thousands of years people have used shadow clocks to tell the time. These clocks use the movement of the shadow produced by the Sun. Sundials are shadow clocks.

Mechanical clocks have a device called a regulator, which moves at a steady rate. It turns the hands of the clock through a system of **gear** wheels. Electronic clocks are controlled by the tiny movements of crystals of quartz.
See also **watch.**

▷ In this transparent (see-through) clock, you can see the system of gear wheels that turns the hands.

coach

See **bus.**

coal

Coal is a quite hard, black substance that we burn. It is a **fossil fuel.** It is mined throughout the world. Coal is made up mainly of carbon, with water and dirt. The best coal is anthracite, which is nearly all carbon. When coal is heated strongly without air, it turns into coke. This is used as fuel in **blast furnaces.**

cog wheel

A cog wheel has tiny teeth, or cogs, around its outside edge. Cog wheels are used in **gear** systems and, with chains, for passing on power.

▷ Cog wheels pass on motion (movement) to one another when their teeth lock together.

combine harvester

A combine harvester is a farm machine. It is used to harvest cereal crops, such as wheat and barley. It is so called because it combines the actions of cutting the crop and then beating the grain from it.

commercial vehicle

A commercial vehicle is a road vehicle that is used for work. The most common one is the lorry. Other commercial vehicles include buses, dustcarts, fire engines and tip-up trucks.
See also **lorry.**

▷ A combine harvester has a rotating reel at the front to help collect the cut crop into the machine.

Communications

Communications are ways in which we keep in touch with people, share information and find out what is happening in the world around us. We communicate mainly by speaking and by writing and reading. With the help of modern technology, we can now communicate with each other over long distances, for example by telephone, fax or e-mail.

The electric telegraph was the first reliable method of 'instant' long-distance communications. It was developed in the 1830s, in Britain and in the United States. Messages were sent along wires in the form of electrical signals. The signals stood for words and numbers in a code, usually the **Morse code**. The telephone was invented in 1876 by Alexander Graham Bell in the United States. Fax machines have become popular only in recent years. An even more modern method of communication is electronic mail, or e-mail for short, which uses computers to send messages.

The telephone, fax and e-mail are ways of sending personal communications between a small number of people. Other forms of communications, such as printing and broadcasting, reach millions of people. They are examples of mass communications.

Millions of people read printed newspapers and tune in to radio and television programmes every day.

communications satellite

A communications satellite is a spacecraft that passes on, or relays, communications signals. These signals may be telephone calls, television programmes, fax messages or computer information.

This communications satellite far out in space receives and sends out radio signals from countries all over the world.

▷ This is a picture of Alexander Graham Bell in 1892, speaking on one of his telephones.

▽ With a mobile phone, you can keep in touch with people while moving from place to place.

e-mail

E-mail is short for electronic mail. It is a method of sending letters using computers and a communications network like the Internet. You write a letter on your computer and, using a code, address it to the person you want to contact. You can then send the letter, using the telephone line, directly to that person's computer. If the person's computer is switched off, your electronic letter is 'dropped in the mailbox', or put in the memory of a central computer. The person can use a password to open the mailbox and pick up the letter.

▷ *A fax machine is connected to a telephone line. You press the number buttons to contact the person who will receive the fax. Then you press the green button to send the fax.*

fax

A fax machine sends written messages, documents and pictures along telephone lines. The word 'fax' is short for facsimile, which means an exact copy. A fax machine changes words and pictures into signals. These travel along telephone lines to another fax machine, which reads the signals and then prints out the original words and pictures.

Internet

The Internet is an international communications network. It joins together millions of computer users around the world. Through the network, you can send letters to other users by e-mail. You can also reach huge stores of information, on all kinds of subjects, that are provided by individual people and by organizations.

telephone

The telephone has been the most popular method of personal communications for over 100 years. Today, more than 600 million phones are in use across the world. Many people carry a mobile phone when they move around. Mobile phones are connected to the ordinary telephone network by **radio.** With a videophone, you can see the person you are calling at the same time as you hear them.

telex

The telex is a modern version of the electric telegraph. It sends written messages in the form of electrical signals.

map projected onto back of studio

▽

Television newscasters read out the latest news from around the country and from around the world. They read from notes and from a tele-prompt, which is attached to the TV camera.

sports newscaster

chief newscaster

laptop computer

TV camera

camera operator

tele-prompt

telephone

microphone

TV set

two-way radio

computer

A computer is an electronic device that handles all kinds of information. Computers are used in every part of our lives – in homes, schools, businesses, shops, science, industry and transport. We use them to play games, draw graphs, send electronic mail, keep records of goods, forecast the weather, run chemical plants, fly aeroplanes and much more. They are a central part of **information technology.**

The data stored in the memory and the program of instructions form part of the computer's software.

You feed data into a computer in the form of words and numbers. The computer automatically changes the words and numbers into a code made up of sets of 0s and 1s, or **bits.**
See also **communications, disk, word processing.**

A computer stores information, or data, in its memory. It then handles, or processes, the data by following a set of instructions, called a program. The part of the computer that carries out the instructions is called the processor, or central processing unit (CPU).

The memory and CPU are made up of **microchips.** They are part of the computer's hardware. Other items of hardware include a keyboard, a mouse, a computer screen, or visual display unit (VDU), a disk drive, a printer and a **modem.**

The keyboard and mouse are 'input' devices (for putting information into the computer). The VDU, printer and modem are 'output' devices (for taking information from the computer).

concrete
See **materials.**

conservation
Conservation means taking care of, or preserving, something. The conservation of resources, such as minerals and fossil fuels, and the conservation of wildlife are very important in the modern world. If we carry on using up resources too quickly, there will be none left for the future.
See also **fossil fuel, materials, recycling.**

conveyor

A conveyor carries, or conveys, objects or materials. A conveyor belt is an endless band of material that is looped around a set of **pulleys.** In a roller conveyor, objects move over a row of rotating (turning) rollers. Both kinds of conveyor are used widely in factories.

△ A worker inspects newly made pasta as it passes by on a conveyor belt.

cracking

Cracking is one of the most important chemical processes that takes place at an **oil refinery**. It breaks down thick oils into more useful products, such as petrol and chemicals for use in industry.

crane

A crane is a machine for lifting and moving heavy loads. The load is carried by a hook at the end of a wire rope, or cable. The cable is let out and wound back by a power-driven **winch.**

crude oil

See **petroleum.**

dam

A dam is a thick strong wall built to hold back water. The artificial lake trapped behind the dam is called a reservoir. Dams are built of concrete or a mixture of earth and rock. Very thick dams are called gravity dams because their weight holds back the water. Slimmer concrete dams have an arch shape to hold back the water.
See also **hydroelectric power.**

▷ This is the Hoover Dam on the Colorado River in the western United States. It is an arch dam made of concrete, and is 221 metres (m) high.

data

Data means information. Computers handle, or process, data, for example sorting and updating records. A database is a huge store of information about a particular subject, such as airline timetables. See also **computer.**

jib

cable

pulley

winch

cable

winch

counterweight

trolley

pulley

▷ In a jib crane (near left), the cable hangs from an arm (jib) that can move up and down and from side to side. In a tower crane (far left), the cable hangs from a trolley that travels along a horizontal arm.

design

To design something means to draw up a plan of it. Every object, from a pencil to an ocean liner, has to be designed before it can be made or built.

In technology, a design must be practical and suitable for its planned use. A jug, for example, must be designed so that it pours without dripping, and has a handle that you can hold easily. Designers try to design the jug so that it looks attractive. They must also choose a suitable material to make it.

Even when a design works well, looks good and is made of the right material, it may cost so much to make that people will not be able to afford to buy it.

Designers draw sketches of their designs and often build models to show exactly what the designs will look like. Sometimes they test the models to find out how well they work. Aircraft designers, for example, test their designs in huge **wind tunnels**.

Hot liquid plastic is shaped into a tube as it is forced through the hole in a die.

pellets of plastic

heater

turning screw

die

liquid plastic

plastic tube

desk-top publishing

Desk-top publishing, or DTP for short, means producing printed material with a computer and a printer. Many companies and individuals now use DTP to print and publish their own reports, newsletters and booklets. They prepare the words on the computer using a word-processing program. They plan, or lay out, the pages on the computer's screen using a DTP program. The pages, with their pictures, are then printed by the printer.
See also **computer, word processing.**

developing

See **film.**

die

A die is a kind of mould. It is used to shape metals and other materials. Hot metal or plastic is forced through a die to make tubing, for example.
See also **moulding.**

diesel engine

A diesel engine is an engine that burns a light oil called diesel as fuel. Many cars, trains and ships and most lorries and buses have diesel engines.

A diesel engine works in a similar way to a **petrol engine**. Unlike petrol engines, diesel engines do not need an electric spark to burn the fuel. The air in the cylinders becomes so hot that the fuel burns straight away when it meets the hot air. It then produces hot gases that move the **pistons**.
See also **engine, internal combustion engine.**

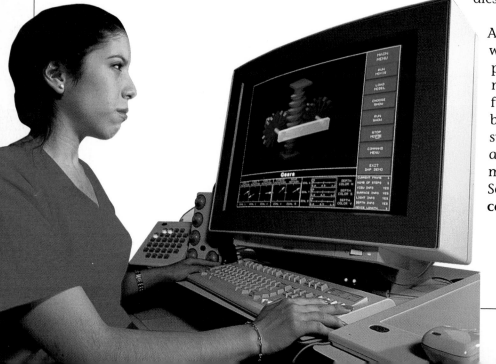

Many manufacturers now use computers to help them design new products. This is known as computer-aided design, or CAD for short.

disk

Computer data and programs are usually stored on disks. The disks are magnetic. Disks that are built into the computer are called hard disks. Floppy disks are portable and bendy. They fit into a slot at the front of the computer called a disk drive.
See also **computer**.

doorbell

An ordinary doorbell uses electricity to make it ring. The electric bell works by using batteries. The main part of the bell is an **electromagnet**. When you press the doorbell button, electricity flows through the electromagnet. It makes a metal clapper hit the bell.

drag

Drag is a force that slows down an object when it moves through a liquid or a gas. It is a kind of **friction**. The drag of the air slows down cars and aeroplanes, and the drag of the water slows down boats.
See also **air resistance, streamlined**.

drill

See **tool**.

drilling rig

Engineers use a drilling rig to drill holes in the ground or seabed when searching for oil. The rig is a tall steel tower with lifting equipment to raise a series of pipes, called the drill pipe. A cutting tool, called a drill bit, is fitted to the bottom of the drill pipe.
See also **petroleum**.

drug

A drug is a substance that is used in medicine to treat or prevent illnesses and to reduce pain. Some drugs are made from plants. Morphine, which is a powerful painkiller, is made from certain poppies. Aspirin is a milder painkiller. Like most drugs, it is made from chemicals. Antibiotic drugs are made from tiny living things such as moulds.

object not streamlined

unsteady air flow causes drag

Chunky objects (top) experience a lot more drag than smooth, streamlined ones (bottom) when they travel through air or water.

smooth air flow

streamlined object

dye

A dye adds colour to textiles, hair, food and other materials. Some dyes, such as madder (red) and indigo (blue), are made from plants. Most dyes are **synthetics**.

An Indian worker dyes a dress a beautiful red colour. The red dye gets into the fibres of the dress fabric.

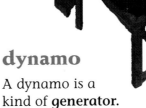

dynamo

A dynamo is a kind of **generator**.

E

echo-sounder

Boats and ships use an echo-sounder to measure the depth of water below them. The instrument works by **sonar**. It sends sound waves down to the seabed, and picks up the echoes that come back. The depth of the water is calculated by measuring the time it takes for the sound waves to reach the seabed and be reflected back to the surface.

echo

sonar
equipment

sound
wave

The echo-sounder on a boat sends out sound waves. The waves are reflected back by the seabed and anything on it.

electric cell

An electric cell produces electricity. The ordinary dry batteries that we use in torches and radios are electric cells.
See also **battery, photocell, solar cell.**

electric generator

See **generator.**

electricity supply

The electricity supply comes into our homes from power stations far away. It travels to us through a huge network of overhead wires, called transmission lines, and underground cables. Tall towers called pylons carry the lines from the power stations to smaller substations all around the country. The substations then pass on the electricity through cables to nearby homes and factories.

electric light

See **fluorescent lamp, light bulb, neon light.**

electric motor

Electric motors power all kinds of machines, from electric toothbrushes and vacuum cleaners to submarines and locomotives. An electric motor is made up of two main parts. One is a rotating part called the rotor. The other is a fixed, or stationary, part called the stator. The stator is a magnet. The rotor carries many coils of wire. It rotates when electricity is passed through the coils.

electromagnet

An electromagnet is a kind of magnet that only becomes magnetic when electric current passes through it. Most electromagnets are made of a piece of iron with coils of wire wrapped around the iron.

electronics

When you switch on a torch, electricity from a battery flows through a light bulb and makes it glow. The electricity is being carried by millions of tiny parts, or particles. We call them electrons.

Electronics studies the flow of electrons in materials. Engineers have developed various parts, or components, to control electrons. They group these components together to build up electronic circuits. Such circuits are found in radios, television sets, computers, calculators, digital watches, CD players, automatic cameras and many other devices.

Thousands of tiny components and circuits can be built up on one tiny piece, or chip, of a material called silicon. This produces a **microchip.** Microchips are so small and powerful that they have made it possible to build electronic devices such as the personal computer (PC).

A simple electric motor. The rotor spins round when electricity from the battery passes through its coils.

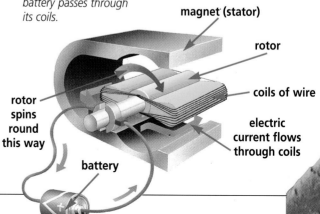

magnet (stator)

rotor

coils of wire

electric current flows through coils

rotor spins round this way

battery

electron microscope

An electron microscope uses beams of electrons (tiny particles that carry electricity) to magnify things. It contains **electromagnets** that bend the electron beams. Electron microscopes can magnify things by up to one million times, which is much more than ordinary light microscopes can. See also **microscope**.

This is how a knot of human hair appears when you look at it through a scanning electron microscope. This kind of electron microscope looks at the surface of objects.

electroplating

Electroplating is a process that uses electricity to cover, or coat, one metal with another. Many car parts are plated with a metal called chromium. Some cutlery is silver plated.

e-mail

See **communications**.

endoscope

An endoscope is an instrument that doctors use to see inside the human body. It is made of bendy glass fibres, and can pass through narrow places and around corners.

engine

An engine is a machine that produces power to drive other machines. Steam engines, **petrol engines** and **diesel engines** use heat to produce power. **Turbines** are engines with rotating wheels. The wheels are spun round by a liquid, such as water, steam or a gas. See also **internal combustion engine, jet engine, steam engine.**

engineering

In engineering, science is put to work. Civil engineers design and build roads, bridges, dams and tunnels. Mechanical engineers design and build machines. Chemical engineers design and build chemical plants.

escalator

An escalator is a moving staircase. The steps are carried on an endless belt. They fold flat at the top and bottom to let people get on and off more easily.

An endless belt carries the steps of an escalator. Another endless belt acts as a handrail for passengers.

handrail

step

electric motor

drive wheel

drive belt

returning steps

excavator

An excavator is a machine for digging into the ground. Some large excavators dig up soil by dragging huge buckets across the ground.

explosive

An explosive is a chemical that explodes violently. When it is set off, large amounts of heat and gas are produced. The gas expands quickly and causes a big blast, which can shatter things. Dynamite and TNT are two very powerful kinds of explosive.

F

factory

See **making and manufacturing.**

fax

See **communications.**

This ferry carries passengers between Manhattan and Staten Island, in the harbour of New York City, USA.

ferry

A ferry is a boat or ship that carries passengers and cargo on journeys across water. A ferry may be an ordinary ship, a **hovercraft** or a **hydrofoil.**

fibre

See **materials.**

fibreglass

Fibreglass is a common material that is used to make items such as sailing boats and fireproof clothing. It is made of plastic that is strengthened with tiny threads, or fibres, of glass.

file

See **tool.**

film

In photography, the pictures taken by a camera are recorded on a film. The film is a ribbon of clear plastic. It is coated with chemicals which are affected by light. When a pattern of light falls on the film, the chemicals are changed. They form a kind of invisible image, or picture, on the film. When the film is developed, it is treated with certain chemicals. The invisible image then becomes visible.
See also **camera, movie.**

taking a picture

invisible image on film

developing the paper

developing the film

projecting film image onto photographic paper

final photographic print

Various stages of developing and printing are needed to turn a film into photographs.

flash gun

A flash gun produces a flash of very bright light. It is used in photography when the natural light is not bright enough to take pictures.
See also **camera**.

floppy disk

See **disk.**

fluorescent lamp

A fluorescent lamp is a kind of electric light. It has a glass tube that glows and gives out light. The tube is filled with gas. When electricity passes through the gas, it gives off invisible rays. These rays strike a white coating inside the tube and it gives out white light.

food technology

Food technology is all the processes that the food industry uses to produce the foods we eat. Some processes in food technology have changed little over the years. Bread and dairy products, for example, are still an important part of the diet in many countries. Bread is made from flour, which is produced by grinding grains of wheat. Butter and cheese are made by processing milk.

Newer food technologies have introduced, for example, margarines and low-fat spreads to replace butter. They are made not from milk but from other fats and oils, such as sunflower oil. Plant oils are also used for cooking. They are obtained from seeds by crushing them.

Another aspect of food technology is food preservation. This means preventing food from rotting. Early ways of preserving food, such as drying it or smoking it over a fire, are still used as well as modern methods, like canning and freezing. In canning, we seal food in cans to keep out the air and germs. In freezing, we keep foods at low temperatures to stop the processes that rot them.

Cheese-making is an old food technology. Workers make cheese by curdling milk, which involves treating the milk so that it becomes a solid called curd.

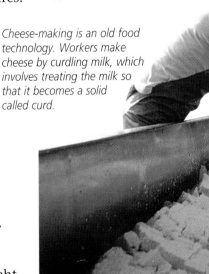

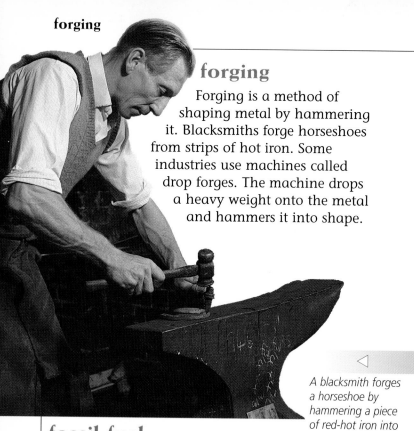

forging

Forging is a method of shaping metal by hammering it. Blacksmiths forge horseshoes from strips of hot iron. Some industries use machines called drop forges. The machine drops a heavy weight onto the metal and hammers it into shape.

◁ *A blacksmith forges a horseshoe by hammering a piece of red-hot iron into shape on an anvil.*

fossil fuel

The fossil fuels are coal, petroleum (crude oil) and natural gas. They are the remains of living things. Coal is the remains of huge trees and ferns that grew up to 300 million years ago. Petroleum and natural gas are the remains of tiny living things from ancient seas.
See also **coal**, **natural gas**, **petroleum**.

foundations

The foundations are at the very bottom of a building or other structure. They support the weight of the building and stop it sinking into the ground. Most foundations are built underground and are made from concrete.

▷ *The foundations of some buildings rest on concrete columns, called piles. These go deep into the ground.*

raft of concrete

concrete pile

four-stroke cycle

See **petrol engine**.

freezing

See **food technology**.

friction

Friction is a force that acts when two surfaces rub together. It tries to stop them moving. It also produces heat. Oil is added to the moving parts of machines to reduce friction.
See also **bearing**, **brake**.

fuel

Fuels are burned to produce heat. Wood has been an important fuel for thousands of years. Today, coal, petroleum (crude oil) and natural gas are our most important fuels.
See also **fossil fuel**, **nuclear energy**.

fuel cell

A fuel cell is a kind of battery. It produces electricity directly from fuel gases without burning. The space shuttle uses fuel cells to produce electricity.

furnace

A furnace burns fuel to produce heat. In the home, small furnaces heat water in a boiler for the hot-water and central heating systems. Large furnaces are used in industry, particularly for smelting metals.
See also **blast furnace**, **central heating**.

galvanizing

Galvanizing means coating steel with a thin layer of zinc. The layer of zinc stops the steel underneath from rusting.

gas

See **natural gas.**

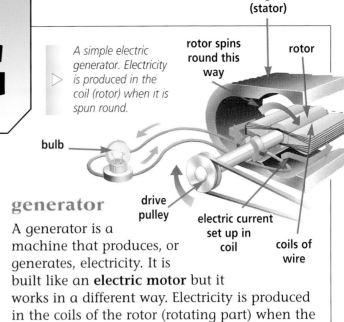

A simple electric generator. Electricity is produced in the coil (rotor) when it is spun round.

magnet (stator)

rotor spins round this way

rotor

bulb

drive pulley

electric current set up in coil

coils of wire

generator

A generator is a machine that produces, or generates, electricity. It is built like an **electric motor** but it works in a different way. Electricity is produced in the coils of the rotor (rotating part) when the rotor spins round.

genetic engineering

Genetic engineering means changing the make-up of living things, or organisms. Genetic engineers alter an organism's genes, which are the tiny parts that control what it is like. In this way they produce better medicines and crops. See also **biotechnology.**

geothermal power

Geothermal power is produced by using the heat inside the Earth. It is a kind of **alternative energy.** Most geothermal power stations are built near volcanic areas, where the underground rocks are hot. When water trickles into the hot rocks, it heats up and turns to steam. The steam is piped to power stations.

girder

See **beam.**

glass

See **materials.**

glider

A glider is an aeroplane without an engine. It flies by 'riding' on currents of air. Another name for glider is sailplane. Gliders are launched from the ground by a powerful **winch,** or towed into the air by an aeroplane powered by an engine.

This motorist is using a pressure gauge to check the pressure of the air in his car tyres.

gauge

A gauge is used to measure things.

The gauge of a wire or tube means its width, or diameter.

The gauge of a railway track is the distance between its rails.

gear

Gears are used in machines to pass on, or transmit, power and movement from one part of the machine to another. A gear is usually a set of wheels with teeth around the outside edges. The teeth of one wheel fit into the teeth of another wheel. So when one wheel turns, it makes the other turn too. If the second wheel has a different number of teeth from the first, it will be driven round at a different speed. See also **cog wheel.**

global warming

Global warming is the gradual heating-up of the Earth's climate. Scientists think that global warming is being caused by an increase in the **greenhouse effect**.

glue

Glue is a liquid used for sticking things together. It is one kind of **adhesive**. Glues are made out of natural materials such as fish bones and animal bones and hides (skins).

gramophone

See **record player**.

greenhouse effect

The layers of air around the Earth trap some of the heat we receive from the Sun. We call this process the greenhouse effect. These layers, known as the atmosphere, trap the heat like a garden greenhouse. Scientists think that the greenhouse effect is increasing because heavy gases are building up in the atmosphere. This increases the temperature of the Earth. See also **global warming**.

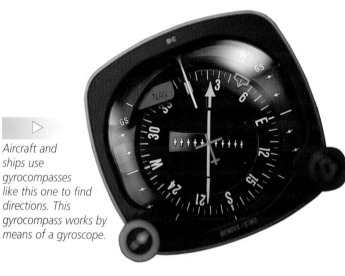

▷
Aircraft and ships use gyrocompasses like this one to find directions. This gyrocompass works by means of a gyroscope.

gyroscope

A gyroscope is a spinning wheel set inside a frame. When it spins, a gyroscope wheel always points in the same direction. For this reason it is used in compasses to show directions.

H

half-tone process

The half-tone process is used to print copies of paintings and photographs. It breaks up the painting or photograph into a pattern of tiny dots. This pattern is then copied onto printing plates.
See also **printing**.

hammer

See **tool**.

hardware

See **computer**.

helicopter

A helicopter is an aircraft that can fly in any direction. It can also hover in the air like a hummingbird. There is a set of rotating blades, called the rotor, on top of the helicopter. When the rotor blades spin round, they produce forces that lift the helicopter in the air and move it.

Helicopters also have a small rotor at the back, or tail. The tail rotor stops the helicopter from spinning round when the main rotor turns.

hi-fi

Hi-fi is short for high-fidelity. A hi-fi sound system, such as a record player or tape recorder, reproduces sound that is almost as good as the original sound.

hologram

A hologram is a picture made by a **laser** beam. It does not look flat like an ordinary picture. We call a hologram a three-dimensional (3D) picture because it seems to have depth.

hot-air balloon

See **balloon**.

propelle

rudder

engines

lift fan

air cushion

hovercraft

A hovercraft is a vehicle that glides over the surface of land or water on a cushion of air. It is sometimes called an air-cushion vehicle (ACV). A powerful fan forces air under the hovercraft to produce the cushion. Hovercraft are driven forwards by **propellers**.

△

A hydroelectric power station in California, USA. The water stored behind the dam is used to turn the generators that produce electricity.

hydraulic power

Hydraulic power is the force that is carried by a liquid, usually an oil. The foot brake in a motor car works by hydraulic power. When the driver presses down the brake pedal, liquids in pipes carry the pressure to the brakes.

▽

A hovercraft that travels over the sea has a 'skirt' to trap the air underneath. This makes a deeper cushion of air.

hydroelectric power

Hydroelectric power (HEP) is electricity that is produced by using the energy in flowing water. In a typical hydroelectric power station, water from a reservoir is pumped to water **turbines.** It turns the turbines. They drive electric **generators** to make electricity.
See also **power station**.

hydrofoil

A hydrofoil is a boat that skims across the surface of the water. It is fitted with underwater wings called foils. When the foils move through water, they lift the body, or hull, of the hydrofoil above the surface. It can now travel much faster because it is free from the resistance of the water.
See also **drag.**

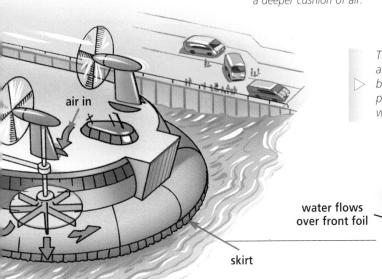

air in

skirt

▷ *This hydrofoil has foils at the front and back. It is unusual because it is driven by powerful jets of water.*

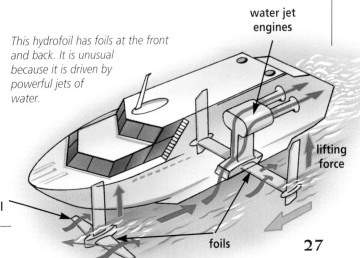

water jet engines

lifting force

water flows over front foil

foils

I

Industrial Revolution

The Industrial Revolution is a period of history when people first worked in factories. At this time, they began to use machines to produce goods. At first the machines were driven by water power, and then later by steam engines. The Industrial Revolution began in Britain in the mid-1700s and soon spread to other countries.

industry

Industry is organized working. Mining is an industry which takes raw materials out of the ground. Some industries make these raw materials into other materials, such as steel or chemicals. Other industries may take steel and chemicals and make them into different materials for other industries, or into finished goods to sell.
See also **making and manufacturing**.

information technology

Information technology (IT) is the handling of information by computer systems. It includes **word processing** and **desk-top publishing**. In banks, shops and businesses, IT is used to move sums of money from one place to another. This activity is known as electronic funds transfer (EFT).
See also **communications, computer**.

internal combustion engine

An internal combustion engine burns fuel inside the engine itself. Petrol engines and diesel engines are examples of internal combustion engines. Steam engines are external combustion engines because they burn fuel outside the engine.
See also **diesel engine, petrol engine**.

Internet

See **communications**.

invention

An invention is a completely new object or idea. Usually it refers to a new machine or other device. One of the greatest inventions ever was the wheel, which was invented in about 3500 BC.

Many inventions, such as television and the motor car, come about gradually as the result of many people's work. Other inventions are the work of just one person, for example Alexander Graham Bell's telephone and Edwin Land's Polaroid 'instant' camera.
See also **communications**.

iron and steel

See **blast furnace, steel-making**.

Information technology helps you to collect money from a cashpoint machine. The machine is connected to your bank so that you can take money out of your bank account.

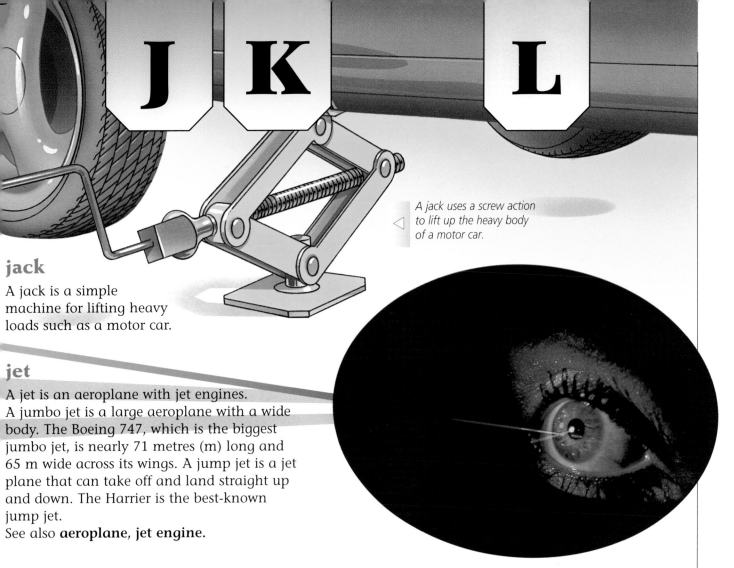

J K L

A jack uses a screw action to lift up the heavy body of a motor car.

jack

A jack is a simple machine for lifting heavy loads such as a motor car.

jet

A jet is an aeroplane with jet engines. A jumbo jet is a large aeroplane with a wide body. The Boeing 747, which is the biggest jumbo jet, is nearly 71 metres (m) long and 65 m wide across its wings. A jump jet is a jet plane that can take off and land straight up and down. The Harrier is the best-known jump jet.
See also **aeroplane, jet engine.**

jet engine

A jet engine is an engine that produces a stream, or jet, of gases. Most aircraft are now powered by jet engines. The jets of gases move, or propel, the aircraft through the air.

The simplest kind of jet engine is called a turbojet. It has three main parts – a compressor, a combustion chamber and a **turbine**. The compressor takes in air and forces it into the combustion chamber. Fuel is burned in the chamber. This produces hot gases which spin the turbine. The gases then escape as a jet out of the back of the engine.

key

See **lock.**

kiln

A kiln is a kind of oven. Pottery is baked hard, or 'fired', in a kiln. **Cement** is made in kilns.

Surgeons sometimes use laser beams to carry out delicate operations on people's eyes.

laser

A laser is an electronic device that produces a powerful beam of light. The beam is very narrow and does not spread out like an ordinary beam of light. Some laser beams are powerful enough to melt and to cut metal. They can be used for **welding.**
See also **CD.**

lathe

A lathe cuts and shapes metal parts. It is one of the commonest **machine tools** in industrial workshops. A sharp cutting tool is forced against a piece of metal to be shaped while it is being turned, or rotated. This process is called turning.

LCD

LCD stands for liquid crystal display. It is the kind of display that you see on digital watches and pocket calculators. An LCD is made up of strips that contain a liquid crystal. This is a kind of liquid plastic that behaves like a crystal. When electricity passes through the strips, the liquid crystal stops light from passing through, so the strips look black.

This pocket organizer has an LCD screen. The letters and numbers on the screen are made up of different arrangements of tiny black strips.

lever

A lever is a very simple machine. It is a **beam**, which rests and turns on a fixed point. This point is called the pivot or fulcrum. A see-saw is a simple lever with the pivot in the middle. A crowbar is a lever with the pivot close to one end. You pull on the handle with a certain force (your effort) to move a heavy load at the end.

life-support system

See **space technology**.

lift

A lift carries people and goods up and down, usually inside tall buildings. It moves inside a space called a shaft. The passenger car usually hangs from a wire rope that goes around a **pulley** at the top of the shaft. A heavy weight is fixed to the other end of the rope. The pulley is driven round by an electric motor.

light bulb

The electric light bulb is our main source of artificial light. It is a glass bulb that is filled with gas. Inside the bulb is a thin coil of wire called the filament.

liner

A liner is a passenger ship. It has many decks that are built on top of one another.

lock

You use a lock to fasten a door. An ordinary lock has a key. When you insert the right key in the lock, it moves the levers or pins inside the lock so that the key can turn. When the key turns, it moves a bolt forwards to lock the door or backwards to unlock it.

Safes and bank vaults are usually fitted with a combination lock. You have to dial the right set, or combination, of numbers to open it.

When electricity flows through the filament inside a light bulb, it becomes white-hot and gives off light.

base

glass bulb

electricity flow through wire

supports

filament coiled w

gas

locomotive

A locomotive pulls trains on the railways. Most modern locomotives have diesel engines or are powered by electricity. Early locomotives had steam engines. See also **transport**.

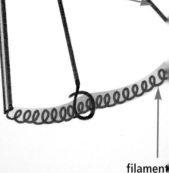

◁

A close-up view of a loom. The threads that you can see are the warp threads. The woven cloth is on the left.

M

machine

Machines do work for us. They help us to carry out all kinds of jobs more easily. They manufacture goods, carry us around and do simple jobs such as opening cans. Simple machines include the **lever** and the **pulley**.

loom

A loom is a machine for weaving cloth. One set of threads (called the weft) is threaded under and over another set of threads (the warp). The warp threads are stretched lengthways on the loom.

lorry

A lorry is a vehicle that carries goods and materials. Lorries are often called trucks. Most lorries have **diesel engines**. Ordinary lorries are built with an all-in-one frame, or chassis. Different kinds of body can be built on this chassis.

machine tool

A machine tool cuts and shapes metal parts. All machine tools have powerful electric motors. The **lathe** is a common machine tool. See also **making and manufacturing**.

maglev

The word 'maglev' is short for magnetic levitation. It is a way of using magnetism to lift an object above a surface. Maglev trains can travel very fast because they are not slowed down by **friction** with the track.

magnetic tape

A magnetic tape is a plastic tape that is coated with magnetic material. It is the kind of tape used in tape recorders and videocassette recorders. Sounds or pictures are recorded on the tape in the form of a magnetic pattern. See also **cassette**.

loudspeaker

A loudspeaker, or speaker for short, is a device that gives out sounds. It turns electrical signals into sound. Speakers are part of sound reproduction equipment, such as tape recorders, record players and radios.

▽

A maglev train in Japan. Magnetism lifts the train a few centimetres above the track.

lubrication

Lubrication usually means oiling. The lubrication system in a car engine supplies oil to the moving parts. The oil helps to reduce **friction**.

MITSUKOSHI HSST

Making and manufacturing

In our daily lives, we buy and use many different things, such as pens and pencils, socks and shirts, pots and pans, bicycles and cars, radios and computers. All these goods have been made in workshops or factories.

Making goods in factories is known as manufacturing. The word 'manufacturing' means making by hand. But in most factories the goods are made by workers using machines.

People have been making things for many thousands of years. The first materials that people used were wood and stone. They used these materials to make tools and weapons. Later, people learned how to bake clay into pottery and smelt minerals into metals. They learned how to mould the clay and cast the metals into shape.

When making a product, first we decide on a suitable design. Then we work out how to make it. Usually, we build it up by joining together, or assembling, simpler parts called components. Then we select suitable materials for the components and suitable tools to shape them. If the product is to be made in a factory, we also have to work out which machines and people will be needed to produce it.

The different stages of building a motor car. First, the car is designed with the help of computers. Then it is put together, piece by piece, on an assembly line.

Robots weld together steel panels to make the body.

Workers fit other body parts, such as the doors.

assembly line

In many factories, workers assemble products from a number of different parts on an assembly line. They stand or sit in line beside a moving **conveyor**. As the product slowly passes by on the conveyor, they add the parts one by one. At the end of the assembly line, the product is complete. The US car maker Henry Ford introduced the moving assembly line in 1913.

More fittings are added to the inside of the car.

Robots spray the body with several coats of paint.

automation

Automation is the use of automatic machines to produce goods or handle industrial processes such as painting or welding. The machines are controlled by computers.

factory

A factory is a place where workers make goods, nearly always by using machines. Work in a factory is very organized. It is split into different jobs, which are carried out by different workers. For example, in a car factory each worker builds only part of a car. Then all the various parts are put together, usually on an assembly line. Because each worker has only one kind of job to do, he or she can learn to do it quickly. This helps to speed up production.

finishing

When something is made in a workshop or a factory, it usually needs finishing in some way before it can be sold or used. For example, a wooden table needs to be varnished or painted. This treatment protects the wood and makes the table look better.

joining

The parts of a product can be joined together in different ways. Wooden parts can be fitted together with the help of carefully cut joints, such as dove tails. They can also be glued, nailed or screwed together. Metal parts can be joined by nuts and bolts. They can be joined more permanently by **soldering** and **welding**.

A Chinese worker finishes a newly made vase by painting a beautiful design on it.

mass production

Mass production means making large amounts of goods in factories. It is possible because factories use machines and efficient methods of working, such as the assembly line.

The final fittings, such as seats and wheels, are added.

shaping

Workers in workshops and factories use various processes to shape the parts or products they make. Cutting is a common process. Carpenters use tools such as knives, chisels and saws to cut wood. Metalworkers use power-driven **machine tools**, which carry out processes such as drilling and milling.

Metalworkers also shape metal by a hammering process called forging. They shape hot liquid metal by **casting** it in moulds. Moulding is a common way of shaping plastics and pottery too. Many pieces of pottery are shaped by hand on a rotating potter's wheel.

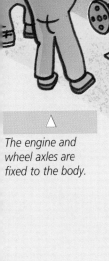

The engine and wheel axles are fixed to the body.

The car is now complete and ready to be driven away.

Materials

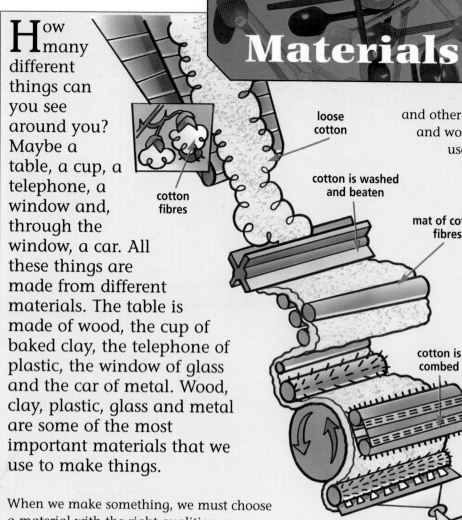

How many different things can you see around you? Maybe a table, a cup, a telephone, a window and, through the window, a car. All these things are made from different materials. The table is made of wood, the cup of baked clay, the telephone of plastic, the window of glass and the car of metal. Wood, clay, plastic, glass and metal are some of the most important materials that we use to make things.

When we make something, we must choose a material with the right qualities, or properties. We make a window out of glass because we can see through glass. It is transparent. We make a car out of metal because metal is strong. We make many objects out of plastic because it is cheap and easy to shape.

ceramic

A ceramic is a material that is made by baking clay and other substances taken out of the ground. Pottery, bricks and tiles are common ceramics. Special ceramics are used for making cooking equipment and cooker hobs. Like many other ceramics, they do not crack or break when you heat them.

concrete

Concrete is a very important building material. It is made by adding water to a mixture of cement, sand and stones. As the mixture dries, it sets hard. Steel bars are sometimes put in concrete to give it extra strength. Then we call it reinforced concrete.

loose cotton

cotton fibres

cotton is washed and beaten

mat of cotton fibres

cotton is combed

cotton rope

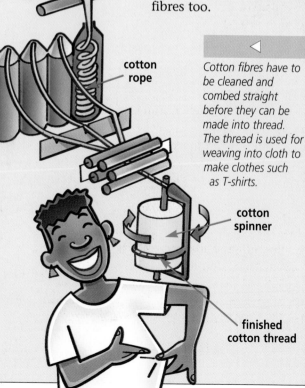

cotton spinner

finished cotton thread

fibre

A fibre is a thin thread. Fibres from plants and animals are used to make cloth and other textiles. Cotton from the cotton plant and wool from sheep are the most widely used natural fibres. **Synthetic fibres** are made from chemicals. They are also widely used in textiles and to make strong materials such as **fibreglass**.

glass

Glass is a hard, transparent (see-through) material. It is cheap to make and easy to shape. It is made by heating sand, limestone and other substances in a **furnace**. The mixture melts into a liquid, which forms glass when it cools.

Liquid glass can easily be shaped into flat sheets for windows. Glass is also shaped into bottles, jars, drinking glasses and other objects. It can be shaped into fine fibres too.

◁

Cotton fibres have to be cleaned and combed straight before they can be made into thread. The thread is used for weaving into cloth to make clothes such as T-shirts.

metal

Most of the metals we use are shiny, hard and strong. Iron, aluminium and copper are our most important metals. We use more iron than all the other metals put together. Iron is used mainly in the form of its **alloy**, steel. Aluminium is useful because it is so light. Copper is used to make electrical wire because it passes on, or conducts, electricity well.

A few metals, such as platinum, gold and silver, are found as metals in the ground. We call them native metals. But most metals are made from minerals.

mineral

A mineral is a chemical substance that makes up rocks. We use many minerals as raw materials. For example, we use limestone to make cement, and sand to manufacture glass. The most important minerals are **ores**, from which we make metals. We can make copper from a mineral called cuprite. It is a copper ore.

plastic

A plastic is a material that can be shaped easily. Plastics are **synthetics**. Most plastics are made from chemicals obtained from petroleum. In general, plastics are light and tough. They do not rust or rot, and they do not conduct electricity.

Common plastics include polythene (polyethene), **PVC** and Teflon. Polythene is used to make bottles, bowls and bags. PVC is used to make floor tiles, guttering and rainwear. Teflon is heat-resistant and is used for the non-stick coating on kitchen pans. Some plastics can be filled with air bubbles to make foams.

Plastic objects like these teaspoons are cheap and easy to make. Also, they can be brightly coloured.

raw material

Raw materials are the basic substances we use to make things. Some of the most important raw materials are minerals, petroleum, wood, and fibres from plants and animals.

wood

Wood from trees has been used for tens of thousands of years, and is still widely used today. We call pieces of wood 'timber'. Most timber is used in buildings to make roofs, floors, doors and so on. Large amounts of wood are used to make paper. See also **paper**.

Wood is still the best material for making some musical instruments, such as guitars.

memory

See **computer**.

metal

See **materials**.

metal fatigue

Metal fatigue can weaken a metal. It happens when the metal has been bent, twisted or stretched over and over again.

metallurgy

Metallurgy deals with metals. It includes the removal, or extraction, of metals from their ores, and how the metals are then refined and shaped. **Casting**, **forging** and **rolling** are different methods of shaping metals.

meter

A meter is a measuring instrument. It refers especially to instruments that make electrical measurements, such as an ammeter which measures electrical current.

microchip

A microchip is a tiny thin piece of a hard substance called silicon. It is sometimes called a silicon chip. It contains thousands of miniature electronic pathways, or circuits. The circuits can be seen only under a microscope.
See also **computer**.

▷

This magnified picture of a microchip shows its different circuits. Microchips are used in computers, calculators, robots and many other machines.

metal plate

coil of wire

magnet

microfilm

Microfilm is a piece of photographic film. It contains tiny images (pictures) of documents, records, newspapers and so on. Many libraries have microfilm readers. These produce a bigger, or magnified, image of the film on a screen.

microphone

A microphone is used to record or broadcast sounds. It turns the sounds into electrical signals. Sound waves enter a microphone and make a thin metal plate shake backwards and forwards, or vibrate. The vibrations are then changed into electrical signals. These signals can be broadcast by radio or television, or recorded on magnetic tape or on a CD.

A cutaway view of a microphone. When you speak or sing into it, the sound of your voice makes the metal plate vibrate. These vibrations set up tiny electrical signals that carry the pattern of your sound. ◁

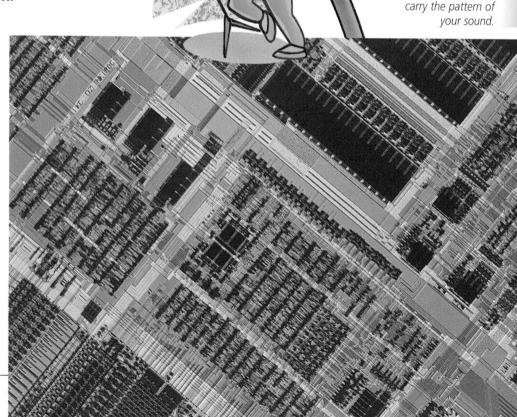

h ••••   i ••   j •---   k -•-   l •-••   m --   n -•

u ••-   v •••-   w •--   x -••-   y -•--   z --••

The letters of the alphabet in the international Morse code.

microscope

A microscope is an instrument that makes tiny objects look much bigger. It uses glass lenses to magnify an object placed on a glass slide. A compound microscope has two lenses – one near the object (the objective) and one near your eye (the eyepiece). You change the position of the two lenses until you can see a clear picture.
See also **electron microscope.**

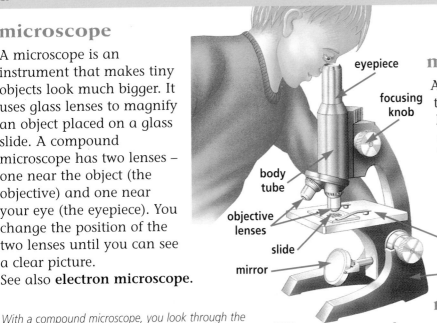

eyepiece
focusing knob
body tube
objective lenses
slide
mirror
stage
stand

With a compound microscope, you look through the eyepiece and the objective at an object on the slide. You turn the focusing knob until you can see the object clearly.

microwave oven

A microwave oven cooks food by using microwaves. These waves are similar to radio waves. The microwaves make tiny drops of water in the food move quickly backwards and forwards, or vibrate. This causes the food to heat up.

mineral

See **materials.**

mining

Mining means digging out coal, metals and minerals from the ground. Gravel and rock are dug out of a **quarry.** Mines on the surface are called opencast mines. In underground mines, vertical shafts and horizontal tunnels have to be dug to reach the coal, metals or minerals.

missile

A missile is any object that is thrown. In warfare, a missile is a weapon with a **rocket motor.** It flies towards its target. Most missiles are guided to their target. Some missiles may be attracted to a target by its heat. Some fly along a **laser** beam. Other missiles follow a detailed map inside the memory in the missile's computer.

modem

A modem is an electronic device that can be fitted to a computer. It allows the computer to send and receive information, or data. The modem changes the computer signals into suitable electrical signals that can travel along telephone lines.
See also **computer.**

monorail

A monorail is a kind of railway. It has just one rail, instead of the usual two. Monorail trains run on top of the track or hang beneath it.

Morse code

The Morse code is used to send messages over long distances. Dots and dashes in the code stand for letters of the alphabet and numbers. They are arranged into coded messages. An American, Samuel Morse, invented the code to send messages on the telegraph, which he also invented.
See also **communications.**

motion picture

See **movie.**

motor

A motor is a machine that changes energy into movement, or motion.
See also **electric motor, engine, rocket motor.**

Here is a message in Morse code. What does it say? (The answer is at the bottom of the page.)

start here

Answer: TAKE ME TO YOUR LEADER

37

motor car

The motor car is our most common means of transport. There are over 400 million cars throughout the world, more than half of them in the United States. The car is one of the most complicated machines we come across in our daily lives. It has up to 14 000 separate parts.

Most cars are powered by a **petrol engine**, but some have a **diesel engine**. The transmission system carries, or transmits, the power from the engine to the wheels that drive the car.

motorway

A motorway is a main road that is specially built for high-speed motor vehicles. It has two sets of lanes that are separated by a central barrier. The barrier keeps apart the traffic travelling in opposite directions. A motorway has no crossroads, roundabouts or traffic lights. Other roads must cross either over or under it.

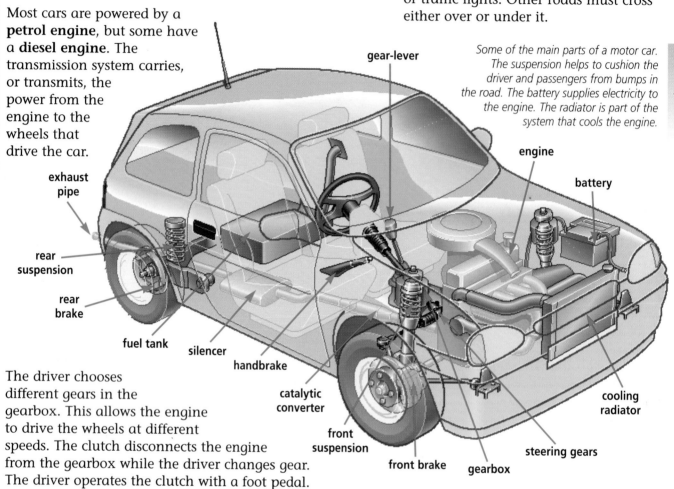

Some of the main parts of a motor car. The suspension helps to cushion the driver and passengers from bumps in the road. The battery supplies electricity to the engine. The radiator is part of the system that cools the engine.

gear-lever

engine

battery

exhaust pipe

rear suspension

rear brake

fuel tank   silencer

handbrake

catalytic converter

front suspension

front brake   gearbox

steering gears

cooling radiator

The driver chooses different gears in the gearbox. This allows the engine to drive the wheels at different speeds. The clutch disconnects the engine from the gearbox while the driver changes gear. The driver operates the clutch with a foot pedal.

Two other foot pedals are used to control the car. One is the accelerator, which controls the speed of the engine. The other is the brake pedal, which the driver presses to put on the brakes. The driver changes direction by turning the steering wheel, which turns the front wheels.

motorcycle

A motorcycle, or motorbike, is a two-wheeled vehicle. It is driven by a **petrol engine**. In most motorbikes, a chain connects the engine with the back wheel and drives it round. In a few motorbikes, the engine drives the back wheel by a rod, or shaft.

moulding

Moulding is a way of shaping materials by pouring or forcing them into moulds. Most plastics are forced into a mould when they are soft or liquid. When they cool and harden, they take the shape of the mould. Plastic bottles are blown into shape in moulds. Plastic bowls are made by injecting melted plastic, under pressure, into moulds. See also **casting**.

mouse

See **computer**.

A piece of film from a movie. Each picture has been taken a tiny part of a second after the picture before it.

movie

A movie is a moving picture like the one you watch in a cinema. It is also called a motion picture or a film. In fact, the pictures in a movie do not move. At the cinema, a **projector** throws a series of still pictures onto the screen. In each picture, anything moving has changed its position slightly. When you look at the cinema screen, all the different pictures blend together in your eyes. You think that the action you see is part of one moving picture.
See also **cine camera**.

multimedia

Multimedia refers to the many different ways of handling and presenting information using a computer. It is a part of **information technology**. A **CD-ROM** is one kind of multimedia device.

In a nuclear power station, heat from the fission process inside the reactor turns water into steam. The steam is then fed to turbines, which drive generators to produce electricity.

natural gas

Natural gas is one of our most important fuels. It is a **fossil fuel**. It is a mixture of methane and a number of other gases.

neon light

Neon lights produce a very bright, red-orange light. They are widely used in advertising signs. The light is a glass tube that contains neon gas. The gas glows when electricity passes through it.

Vivid neon lights brighten up the streets of Hong Kong at night.

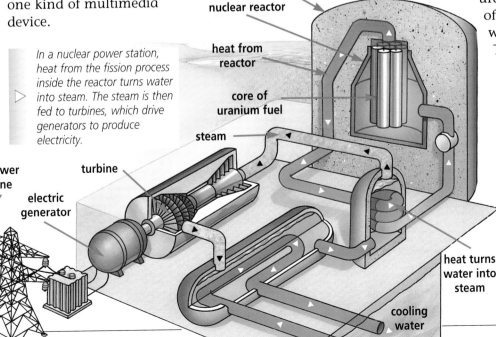

nuclear energy

Nuclear energy is a kind of energy that is locked up inside the centre, or nucleus, of atoms.

Scientists can obtain, or extract, this energy from certain atoms, such as atoms of uranium. A uranium atom gives off huge amounts of energy when its nucleus is split apart. The energy is given off mainly as heat and **radiation**. This process is called fission.

Nuclear energy is also released in another way. This other process is called fusion. In fusion, atoms come together to form a heavier atom. The process of fusion takes place in the Sun and in the stars. It provides the energy to keep them shining.

concrete shield

nuclear reactor

heat from reactor

core of uranium fuel

steam

turbine

electric generator

wer ine

heat turns water into steam

cooling water

nuclear weapon

A nuclear weapon uses nuclear energy to cause very powerful explosions. An atomic bomb is one kind of nuclear weapon. It uses the nuclear energy that is given off when atoms are split. Another kind of nuclear weapon is the hydrogen bomb. It uses the nuclear energy that is given off when atoms of hydrogen join together.
See also **nuclear energy**.

You put oil on metal hinges to let them move easily and to stop them from squeaking.

nut

See **bolt**.

nylon

Nylon is a well-known plastic. It is widely used as a fibre. Nylon was the very first **synthetic fibre**. It was first made in the early 1930s.
See also **material**s.

This scientist is holding an optical fibre. It is carrying a beam of green laser light. Most of the light stays inside the fibre.

offset-litho

See **printing**.

oil

An oil is a greasy liquid that does not mix with water. One kind of oil comes from the ground. We call it crude oil, or petroleum. Other kinds of oil come from animals and plants, for example cod-liver oil and sunflower oil.
See also **petroleum**.

oil refinery

An oil refinery is a place where crude oil is processed. Crude oil, or petroleum, is a mixture of many chemicals. These chemicals are separated out at the refinery. Some of the main products from a refinery are fuels such as petrol, diesel and heating oil, and **petrochemicals**.
See also **cracking**, **refining**.

oil well

See **petroleum**.

optical fibre

An optical fibre is a thin thread of very pure glass. It can carry a beam of light without the light escaping from the sides. Optical fibres are used to make telephone cables. These cables are now replacing copper wires in telephone and other communications systems. They carry electrical signals in the form of **laser** light.
See also **endoscope**.

ore

An ore is a kind of rock. Ores are minerals that contain metal. Magnetite, for example, is a mineral that contains iron. It is a common iron ore. The metals are separated from most ores by **smelting**.
See also **material**s.

organism

An organism is a living thing. Animals, plants, fungi and bacteria are the main kinds of organism. Bacteria are so tiny that you need a microscope to see them. They are called micro-organisms.

P

pacemaker

A pacemaker is a device that is used in medicine. It helps a patient's heart to beat regularly.

paper

Paper is the material on which this book is printed. Most paper is made from wood pulp, which is really a mass of wood fibres. The wood pulp is mixed with water and other materials and is then beaten by machines. The watery pulp flows onto a net of wire, and the water drains away. The thin layer of fibres that remains is dried and then rolled into a smooth sheet of paper.

This X-ray picture shows a pacemaker inside a patient's chest. It sends tiny electrical shocks to the heart muscles.

Paper comes off the paper-making machine as an endless sheet. It is then wound onto a huge reel.

petrochemical

A petrochemical is a chemical that comes from petroleum (crude oil). Petrochemicals are produced in an oil refinery. Many products, such as plastics, paints and dyes, are made from petrochemicals.

petrol

Petrol is a kind of fuel. It is made from petroleum in an oil refinery. Petrol is burned as a fuel in petrol engines.
See also **oil refinery, petrol engine.**

petrol engine

A petrol engine burns petrol as fuel. Most motor cars and motorcycles have petrol engines.
The main part of the engine is a metal block containing a number of round sleeves, called cylinders. Inside each cylinder is a **piston.** A mixture of petrol and air is sucked into each cylinder, one after the other, and burned by an electric spark. The burning produces hot gases that force the pistons down the cylinders.

The pistons are connected to a shaft and make it turn. In a motor vehicle, this turning movement is then passed on to the driving wheels.
See also **internal combustion engine.**

pesticide

A pesticide is a kind of chemical. It kills insects, fungi and other living things that harm crops. The main kinds of pesticides are insecticides (which kill insects), fungicides (which kill fungal diseases) and herbicides (which kill weeds). Herbicides are often called weedkillers. Unfortunately, many pesticides can harm wildlife, and so they must be used with care.

In a petrol engine, each movement of the piston is called a stroke. We say that the engine works on a four-stroke cycle.

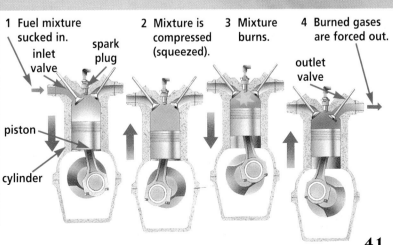

1 Fuel mixture sucked in.
inlet valve
spark plug

2 Mixture is compressed (squeezed).

3 Mixture burns.

4 Burned gases are forced out.
outlet valve

piston

cylinder

petroleum

Petroleum is oil we take out of the ground or from under the sea. We often call it crude oil. It has become the world's most important fuel.

Petroleum is a **fossil fuel**. It is the remains of tiny organisms that lived many millions of years ago. When these organisms died, their bodies rotted and formed a slimy liquid. Over the years, this liquid changed into petroleum. In places, pools of petroleum have become trapped in the layers of rocks. Oil engineers try to find these pools and drill holes down to them. If they find one, the hole becomes an oil well.
See also **drilling rig**.

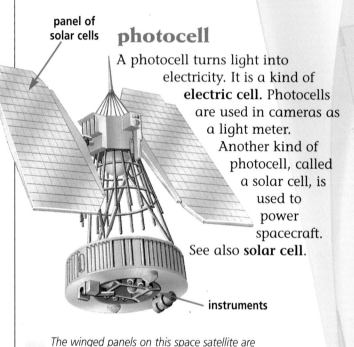

panel of solar cells

photocell

A photocell turns light into electricity. It is a kind of **electric cell**. Photocells are used in cameras as a light meter. Another kind of photocell, called a solar cell, is used to power spacecraft.
See also **solar cell**.

instruments

△ *The winged panels on this space satellite are covered with solar cells, which are a kind of photocell. They turn sunlight into electricity.*

photocopier

A photocopier is a machine that makes copies of pictures and of printed or written words. In a photocopier, the words or pictures on a page are changed into an electrical picture, or image, on a drum. A special ink powder is attracted to this image. The ink is then transferred onto a sheet of clean paper and set by heat.

photography

Photography means taking pictures with a camera.
See also **camera**, **cine camera**, **film**.

piston

A piston is part of an engine. It moves backwards and forwards inside a sleeve, or cylinder. Pistons in cylinders are the most important parts of petrol engines, diesel engines and steam engines. Hot gases or steam force the pistons down the cylinders to produce power.
See also **diesel engine**, **petrol engine**, **steam engine**.

plane

See **tool**.

plans

Plans are a set of drawings that show how something is to be made or built. Sometimes plans show where something is to be positioned. Usually they are drawn to scale. This means that all the things shown in the plans are the right size in relation to one another. In some plans, the lines of the drawings are reproduced as blue lines. These plans are called blueprints.
See also **design**.

plastic

See **materials**.

pliers

See **tool**.

▷ *The plans for a house show what the building will look like. They also give details about how the house will be built.*

plough

A plough is a farm tool that turns over, or tills, the soil. It is pulled by a tractor. Ploughs break up the soil and bury the weeds. They are used to prepare the soil for sowing and planting.

pollution

Pollution means poisoning or causing some kind of harm to our surroundings. The gases that are given out by car engines and factory chimneys cause air pollution. Oil spills from ships can cause pollution of the seas. **Pesticides** can pollute farmland and harm wildlife.
See also **acid rain, greenhouse effect.**

On a plough, curved blades cut into the soil and turn it over.

polymer

A polymer is a kind of material. The word 'polymer' means many parts. Usually, polymer refers to a plastic. Plastics are built up by joining together many groups of atoms, called molecules. So a plastic is a material built up of many parts. Some natural materials are made up of polymers too. For example, wood and cotton are made up of a natural polymer called cellulose.
See also **materials.**

polythene

Polythene is a well-known plastic. Its correct chemical name is polyethene. It is made by heating a gas called ethene (ethylene), which is produced in an **oil refinery**.
See also **materials.**

pottery

Pottery is any object that is made of baked clay. Making pottery is one of the oldest human activities. Since about 5000 years ago, potters have shaped their pottery on a rotating wheel. The three main kinds of pottery are earthenware, stoneware and porcelain. They are made from different clays and are baked, or 'fired', at different temperatures.
See also **kiln, making and manufacturing, materials.**

A potter shapes wet clay into a vase while the clay spins round on a rotating wheel.

power station

A power station is a place where huge amounts of electricity are produced. Hydroelectric power stations produce electricity by using the energy in flowing water. Nuclear power stations use **nuclear energy.** Most power stations use the energy in fuels, such as coal, oil and natural gas. They burn fuels to produce heat, which changes water into steam. The steam is fed to **turbines,** which spin generators to produce electricity.
See also **electricity supply, hydroelectric power.**

pressure cooker

A pressure cooker is a container in which food can be cooked quickly. In an open pan, food cooks at the temperature of boiling water (100 degrees Celsius, or 100°C). When food and water are heated in a pressure cooker, the water reaches a temperature of about 130°C before it boils. The food therefore cooks faster than in an open pan.

printer

A printer is a machine that prints out onto paper the words and pictures from computers. A dot-matrix printer prints letters or numbers as a pattern of dots. An ink-jet printer squirts ink onto the paper from tiny nozzles. A laser printer uses a fine laser beam to form the printed letters and numbers.
See also **computer**.

printing

Printing is the process of making copies of words and pictures, usually on paper. The most common method of printing books and magazines is called offset-litho. In this method printing is done from a flat surface. The type area on the printing plate is treated in a certain way so that it is the only part that attracts printing ink.

probe

See **space technology**.

program

See **computer**.

A worker checks a sheet of paper from a printing press. Both sides of the sheet are printed. Later, the sheets will be cut up and folded to make the pages of a book.

projector

A projector is used to throw, or project, a picture onto a screen. Projectors have two main parts – a powerful light and a lens. The lens is used to enlarge, or magnify, the picture.
See also **movie**.

screen ⟶

propeller

A propeller is used to move an aeroplane or a ship forwards. It is a device with curved blades. It is often called a screw, because it turns round rather like a screw as it travels through the air or water.
See also **screw**.

This is a slide projector for showing colour slides, or transparencies. Its powerful light shines through a slide and throws a large picture onto the screen.

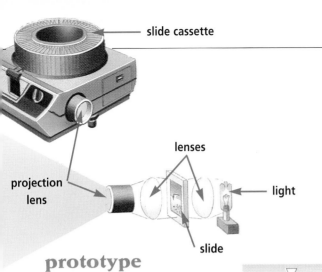

slide cassette

lenses

projection
lens

light

slide

quarry

A quarry is a place where rock, stone and gravel are dug out of the ground. Gravel is dug out in huge quantities and is mixed with cement to make concrete.

prototype

A prototype is an early working example of a machine or some other object. It is usually made in order to test the machine. Aircraft manufacturers, for example, carry out many tests on prototypes to make sure that their designs work well. See also **design**.

pulley

A pulley is a simple lifting machine. Pulleys make it easier to lift heavy loads. A simple pulley consists of a grooved wheel with a rope passing over it.

pump

A pump is used to move liquids and gases. A bicycle pump uses a **piston** to push air into a tyre. In a car, a pump with turning **gears** moves oil through the engine.

PVC

PVC is a common plastic. It is short for polyvinyl chloride. PVC is used to make things such as waterproof clothing, drainpipes, beach balls and the covering, or insulation, around electrical wires.

By using a rope and pulleys, you can move heavy loads more easily.

grooved
wheel

pulleys

rope

heavy
load

radar

Radar is a method of using radio waves to find out where objects are. Air traffic controllers use radar to mark the position of aircraft in the skies. Ships at sea use radar to spot other ships.

In a radar system, an **aerial** sends out beams of very short radio waves, called microwaves. Any object in the path of these waves reflects them back to the aerial as a kind of echo. This echo is displayed on a screen, which shows exactly where the object is.

A ship's radar screen. The screen shows up the coastline and any ships in the area.

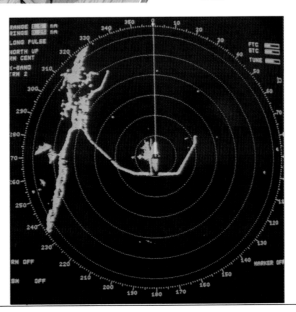

radiation

Radiation means rays. Certain objects give off energy in the form of radiation. Light rays, X-rays and radio waves are some of the many different kinds of radiation. See also **X-ray machine**.

radio

Radio is a way of communicating over long distances. It uses radio waves, which are one kind of **radiation.** The waves can carry electrical signals. These signals may stand for the sounds in radio broadcasting, or the sounds and pictures in television broadcasting.
See also **microphone.**

radio telescope

A radio telescope collects radio signals from outer space. From these signals, astronomers produce pictures of the heavens. Most radio telescopes have a huge metal dish that picks up the signals.

railway

See **transport.**

R & D

R & D stands for research and development. It means thinking up ideas for new products or how to improve existing ones. Many manufacturers have an R & D department. The people who work in it look into, or research, new processes and new materials. If they find something that works well, they may design and build a **prototype.**
See also **making and manufacturing, materials.**

raw material

See **materials.**

recording

See **cassette, CD, record player, tape recorder, videocassette recorder.**

This group of dish aerials in New Mexico, USA, makes up one of the world's largest radio telescopes.

record player

A record player plays back the sound from a thin plastic disc. The disc is called a record. Sounds are recorded on it in a spiral groove.

To play back the sounds, the record is spun round on a turntable. A needle is placed on the record and it moves quickly backwards and forwards, or vibrates, as it follows the groove. The vibrations are changed into electrical signals. These pass to a loudspeaker, which turns them into sounds. A record player is also called a gramophone. Records are no longer so common. They have mostly been replaced by **CDs.**

recycling

Recycling means re-using waste materials. Glass, steel, aluminium, paper and plastics are now recycled in large amounts. Recycling saves materials as well as the energy that is needed to make the materials in the first place.

refining

Refining means making pure. Metals need to be refined after **smelting** because they contain many unwanted substances. Petroleum (crude oil) refining has to take place before the petroleum becomes useful.
See also **oil refinery.**

refractory

A refractory is a material that stands up to, or resists, heat well. Refractories are used, for example, to line furnaces.

refrigerator

A refrigerator is a machine that keeps foods and drinks cool. It uses the scientific idea that something takes in heat when it turns from a liquid into a gas.

In a refrigerator, a cooling liquid flows through pipes around the food compartment. Inside these pipes it changes from a liquid to a gas and takes in heat from the food. The gas then flows to a kind of pump called a compressor. This helps turn the gas back to a liquid. You hear a refrigerator make a noise when the compressor is working.

reservoir

See **dam.**

riveting

Riveting is a way of joining together pieces of metal. It is used in shipbuilding and other construction work. A rivet is a metal pin with a head at one end. The tail end is pushed through holes in the metal pieces to be joined. Then it is hammered to form another head. The metal pieces are firmly held between the two heads.

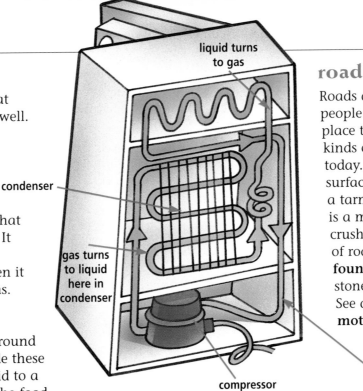

liquid turns to gas

condenser

gas turns to liquid here in condenser

compressor

gas returns to compressor

A look inside a refrigerator, showing the parts that make it work. The cooling substance takes in heat from inside the refrigerator as it changes from a liquid to a gas.

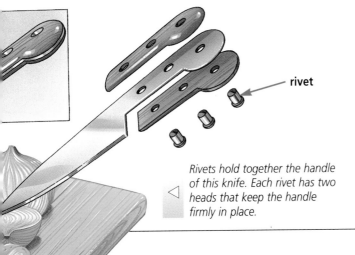

rivet

Rivets hold together the handle of this knife. Each rivet has two heads that keep the handle firmly in place.

road

Roads are built to carry people and vehicles from place to place. Two main kinds of roads are built today. One has a concrete surface, and the other has a tarmac surface. Tarmac is a mixture of tar and crushed stone. Both kinds of roads have **foundations** of crushed stone.
See also **materials, motorway.**

robot

A robot is a machine that is built to do the work of humans. Some robots even look like humans. They are called androids. The robots used in industry have mechanical arms and hands, but they do not look at all like humans. They are now widely used on factory production lines.
See also **making and manufacturing.**

rocket motor

A rocket motor drives a missile or a space rocket forwards. It burns fuel to produce a stream of gases. The gases shoot backwards out of a nozzle at the back of the motor. As the gases shoot out backwards, the rocket is pushed, or propelled, forwards.

Rocket motors can work in space, where there is no oxygen. They carry the oxygen that is needed to burn the fuel. Jet engines take the oxygen they need from the air around them, so they do not work in space.
See also **jet engine, space technology.**

rolling

Rolling is a way of shaping metal. Thick pieces of metal are first heated and then squeezed between heavy rollers.

S

satellite

See **space technology**.

scales

Scales are used to weigh objects. A balance is a pair of scales that weighs very accurately. It is used in chemical laboratories. In some scales the weight of the object moves a lever or stretches a spring. Modern electronic scales have a device called a strain gauge. The object being weighed stretches a wire inside the gauge.

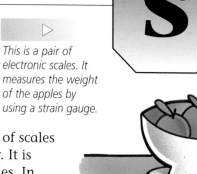

▷ This is a pair of electronic scales. It measures the weight of the apples by using a strain gauge.

screw

A screw is a metal pin that fastens things together. The pin has a spiral groove, or thread. Nuts and bolts also have screw threads.

A screw is a simple machine. A **jack**, for example, uses a screw and a lever to lift up a motor car. An aeroplane or boat **propeller** is another kind of screw.
See also **bolt**.

◁ When you turn a screw, the thread digs into the material you want to fasten.

thread

sewage treatment

Sewage is the watery waste that comes from homes and other buildings. It contains detergents and dirt as well as human waste from lavatories.

Sewage must be cleaned and made safe before it can be allowed back into the environment. It is piped to sewage treatment plants. There the solid matter is separated from the waste and the liquid part is passed through filter beds. In these beds, tiny **organisms** feed on the waste and so help to clean the water. Chemicals may also be added.

shaping

See **making and manufacturing**.

ship

See **transport**.

silicon chip

See **microchip**.

simulator

A simulator is a machine or device that copies, or simulates, another one. Pilots train in a flight simulator. It behaves like a real aeroplane but it never leaves the ground. The inside of the simulator is built to look exactly like the flight deck of an aeroplane. It has the same controls and instruments, but its 'windows' are large computer screens. Astronauts use simulators of spacecraft for training.

seaplane

A seaplane is an aeroplane that takes off from and lands on water. A flying boat is a seaplane with a hull that is shaped like a boat. A float plane has floats instead of wheels.

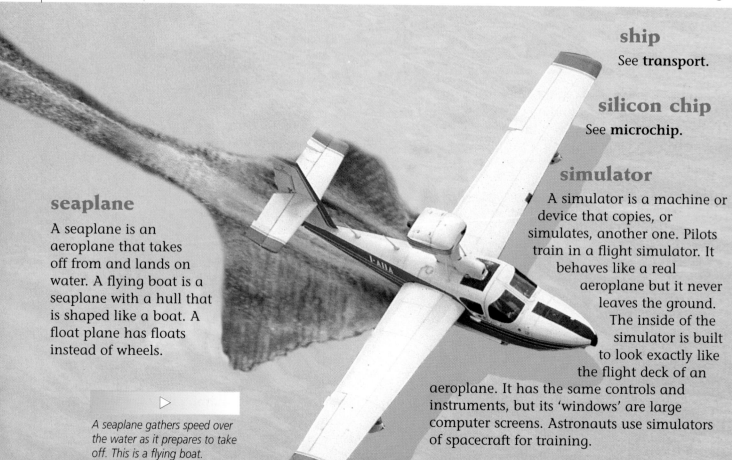

▷ A seaplane gathers speed over the water as it prepares to take off. This is a flying boat.

skyscraper

A skyscraper is a very tall building. It is built with very firm **foundations** to support its heavy weight. Skyscrapers have a very strong frame that is made of steel beams, or girders. The walls 'hang' from this frame. Skyscraper walls do not carry any weight, unlike the walls in ordinary houses. Skyscrapers are made mostly of metal, concrete and glass.

smart card

A smart card is a plastic card, rather like a credit card. It carries a large amount of information. This information is in a **microchip**, which is set in the plastic. Special card readers can read the information that is stored in the microchip.

smelting

Smelting is a process that uses heat to take out, or extract, a metal from its **ore**. Metal is produced when the ore is heated strongly with a substance such as coke. Iron ore, for example, is smelted in a **blast furnace.**

software

See **computer.**

solar cell

A solar cell turns sunlight into electricity. It is a kind of **electric cell.** Most satellites are powered by solar panels that carry thousands of cells. The cells are made of thin slices of a hard substance called silicon.

▷

Tall skyscrapers like these are found in modern cities throughout the world. The tallest skyscraper in the world is the Sears Tower in Chicago, USA, which stands 443 metres (m) high.

solar power

Solar power is produced by using energy from the Sun. This energy is called solar energy. Houses can be heated by solar power. Solar panels on roofs trap the Sun's energy rather like a greenhouse does.

soldering

Soldering is a way of joining metal parts. It uses an **alloy** called solder, which is made of tin and lead and melts easily. In use, the solder is melted and dropped on the parts to be joined. It quickly cools and hardens.

▷

Solar power supplies electricity for this phone box in the desert. The electricity is produced by a panel of solar cells.

sonar

Ships and submarines use sonar to find objects underwater. It is a method of navigation (sailing in the right direction) that uses sound waves. Sonar equipment works in much the same way as **radar.**
See also **echo-sounder.**

Space technology

The Earth we live on is surrounded by layers of air. We call these layers the atmosphere. The atmosphere is not very thick. About 200 kilometres (km) above the Earth's surface there is hardly any air left at all. This is the beginning of space.

Scientists started launching craft into space in 1957, beginning with the artificial satellite *Sputnik 1*. It was launched on 4 October 1957. They used rockets to launch these craft because **rocket motors** are the only engines that can work in space. *Sputnik* and other early spacecraft moved around the Earth along a path known as an orbit. They were Earth satellites. Later, scientists launched space probes that went beyond the Earth and travelled to the Moon, other planets and comets.

In 1961, humans began travelling in space. The first person was a Russian, Yuri Gagarin. The first American was John Glenn, early in 1962. Since then, many men and women have been launched into space. Space travellers are called astronauts, but Russian ones are known as cosmonauts.

ESA

ESA stands for the European Space Agency. It organizes space activities in countries in Europe.

life-support system

All spacecraft that carry astronauts and cosmonauts have a life-support system. This keeps them alive while they are in space. The system supplies the spacecraft's cabin with air, keeps it at a comfortable temperature and removes stale air and smells.

The space shuttle blasts off from the launch pad at the Kennedy Space Center in Florida, USA. In less than 15 minutes, it will be travelling in space.

NASA

NASA stands for the National Aeronautics and Space Administration. It organizes space activities in the United States of America.

probe

A probe is a spacecraft that travels beyond the Earth. Probes visit the Moon and distant planets and comets. They take pictures and collect data (information) and send them back to Earth. Probes have now visited all the planets in the Solar System, except Pluto.

helmet visor

jet-propelled backpack

controls

spacesuit

satellite

A satellite is a spacecraft that circles around the Earth in space. As many as 100 satellites are launched every year. Communications satellites pass on, or relay, telephone, radio and television signals from country to country. Weather satellites keep a watch on the world's weather. Astronomy satellites look into outer space to study stars and galaxies.

spacesuit

A spacesuit protects astronauts when they walk in space. It gives them oxygen to breathe and protects them from heat and cold, and from dangerous rays.

Spacelab

Spacelab is a space laboratory that is carried into space by the space shuttle. It was built by the ESA. Both American and European scientists fly on Spacelab missions. They carry out all kinds of experiments, such as finding out how substances and people are affected by being in space.

This astronaut is ready to go spacewalking. A jet-propelled backpack helps the astronaut to move around outside the spacecraft.

spacewalking

We say that astronauts go spacewalking when they work outside their spacecraft. The proper name for spacewalking is extra-vehicular activity (EVA).

weightlessness

In space, astronauts seem to have no weight. We call this condition weightlessness. It affects everything that the astronauts do, such as eating, sleeping and moving about.

space shuttle

The space shuttle is the main spacecraft that NASA uses to send astronauts into space. It is made up of three parts. The main part, called the orbiter, carries the astronauts. The external tank holds fuel for the orbiter's engines. The solid rocket boosters, or SRBs for short, provide extra power at lift-off. Both the orbiter and the SRBs are used again and again. The four orbiters in the shuttle fleet are *Columbia, Discovery, Atlantis* and *Endeavour*.

Astronauts on board one of the space shuttles took this picture of Russia's space station Mir. It is made up of several units that have been joined together.

space station

A space station is a large spacecraft. Astronauts live and work inside it for months at a time. The Russians have a space station called *Mir*. NASA is planning to build an international space station called *Alpha*.

American astronauts and Russian cosmonauts meet inside the Mir space station in 1995. Mir was launched into orbit in 1986, and people have been living in it ever since.

spanner

See **tool**.

speaker

See **loudspeaker**.

spinning machine

A spinning machine makes thread by twisting together lots of fibres (tiny threads). The thread, or yarn, is used to make cloth. The first simple spinning machine was the spinning wheel, which came into use in the 1300s. In the 1700s, better spinning machines were invented. They helped to make the textile industry the first great industry. All spinning machines do two things. They take masses of short fibres and gather them into a loose rope. Then they draw out and twist this rope into a fine thread. The twist gives the thread extra strength. See also **loom**.

spring

A spring is a machine part that can be bent, pulled or pushed. Afterwards it returns to its original state. Metal coil springs are often used in the suspension system of motor cars.

clockwork spring

sprinkler system

A sprinkler system is fitted inside a building so that it sprays water if a fire breaks out. It consists of water pipes and nozzles. The holes in the nozzles are filled with an **alloy**, which melts at a low temperature. The heat from a fire melts the alloy and allows water to spray out.

expanded spring

△

Coil springs are found in many machines. As the coil springs inside some watches unwind, they provide the power to turn the hands.

stealth plane

A stealth plane is a military aeroplane that is difficult to find in the air. It is specially designed so that it is almost invisible to **radar**. The plane has an unusual shape, with many flat surfaces. Its engine exhausts give off very little heat. This helps the plane to avoid missiles that find their target by looking for heat.

steam engine

A steam engine produces power to drive machinery. Steam engines were the first successful engines. They were the main power source in industry in the 1700s and 1800s, and also on the railways until the middle of this century.

In a steam engine, steam from a boiler forces a **piston** along a sleeve-like cylinder. A connecting rod passes on this movement to the machinery that needs to be driven.

steel-making

Making steel is one of the most important processes in industry. Steel is made from iron, which is our most important metal. It is an **alloy** of iron, small amounts of carbon and other metals. The iron, which comes from **blast furnaces**, has to be refined to make steel. Unwanted substances in the iron are burned out with a jet of oxygen. Some steel is made in electric furnaces.

compressed spring

stereo system

A stereo system is a sound system that reproduces life-like sounds. It often consists of a radio, a **CD** player and a cassette player. Stereo is short for stereophonic, which means sound in depth. We hear sounds in depth because we have a right ear and a left ear. Each ear picks up slightly different sounds, and this provides depth. Stereo systems produce a stereo effect by using right and left **loudspeakers** (or headphones) that give out slightly different sounds.

This stealth plane is called the F-117A. Its odd shape makes it almost invisible on radar. This allows the plane to get close to its target without being spotted.

streamlined

A fish can swim through the water easily because it has a streamlined shape. Aircraft, cars and ships are streamlined so that they can travel through the air or water more easily. Streamlining of cars and aeroplanes reduces the **air resistance** on them, so that they can travel faster and use less fuel.

structure

A structure is something that has been built, or constructed. Bridges and skyscrapers are structures.

Structure also means the way that something is made or put together. Scientists examine the structure of the Earth, for example.

submarine

A submarine is a kind of ship that can travel underwater. The body, or hull, of a submarine has tanks that can be flooded with water. This makes the submarine sink. The tanks can also be filled with air, to make the submarine rise to the surface again.

Submarines have **propellers**. They are driven by diesel engines on the surface, and by electric motors under water. Other submarines are powered by **nuclear energy**. Their propellers are driven by steam **turbines**.

submersible

A submersible is a small submarine.

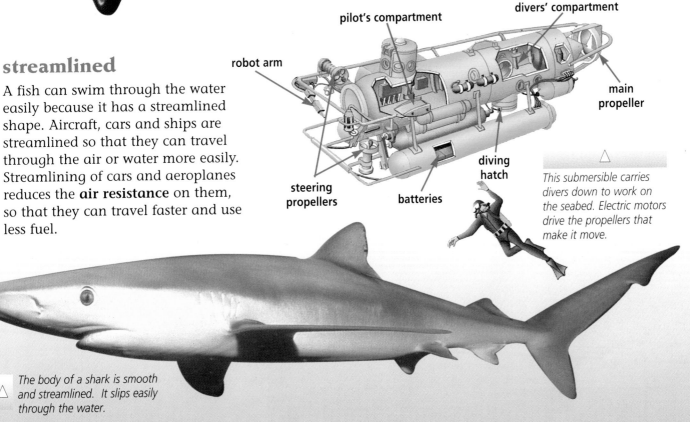

pilot's compartment

divers' compartment

robot arm

main propeller

steering propellers

batteries

diving hatch

This submersible carries divers down to work on the seabed. Electric motors drive the propellers that make it move.

The body of a shark is smooth and streamlined. It slips easily through the water.

supersonic

Supersonic means faster than the speed of sound. Supersonic fighter planes can fly at speeds that are more than three times faster than the speed of sound.

surveying

Surveying is measuring areas of land accurately. Surveyors measure distances, angles and heights. They use an instrument called a theodolite to measure angles. To measure distances, they use electronic instruments called range-finders. These use laser beams or a kind of **radiation** called infrared light.

switch

A switch is used to turn electric current on and off. Light switches are the most common kind of switch. Some are called rocker switches because the part you press rocks backwards and forwards. A dimmer is another kind of light switch.

A construction engineer uses a theodolite to survey a building site. Engineers must survey a site accurately to ensure that the buildings are built in the right place and at the right level.

synthesizer

A synthesizer is an instrument that makes sounds electronically. A music synthesizer can produce the same sound as any other kind of musical instrument. Speech synthesizers can recognize human speech and can also speak words.

synthetic fibre

A synthetic fibre is a thin thread that is made from chemicals. Most synthetic fibres are made from plastics. Very large amounts of synthetic fibres are used in the textile industry, either by themselves or in mixtures with natural fibres such as cotton and wool.
See also **nylon**.

synthetics

Synthetics are materials that have been made from chemicals. They are not made from natural materials such as wood or clay. Plastics are the most common synthetics.
See also **materials**.

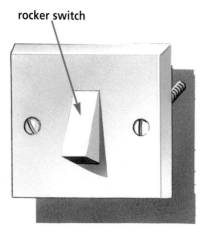

rocker switch

dimmer switch

Two common kinds of light switch. A rocker switch rocks backwards and forwards as it switches the electricity on and off. When you turn a dimmer switch, this lets more or less electricity flow to a light. You can make the light brighter or dimmer in this way.

T

tanker

A tanker is a big ship or lorry that carries large quantities of liquids. The largest oil tankers are more than 500 metres (m) long and can carry half a million tonnes of oil. Tanker lorries carry liquids such as milk, petrol and liquid chemicals.

This tanker carries its cargo of oil in many tanks that are built into its hull (body). The tanker's engine and crew quarters are right at the stern (back).

tape recorder

A tape recorder is a machine that records and plays back sounds. During recording, a microphone changes sounds into electrical signals. These are then changed into magnetic signals, and are recorded on **magnetic tape**. During playback, the magnetic signals are changed back to electrical signals. These are fed to a **loudspeaker**, which reproduces the original sounds. A personal stereo can be a small portable tape recorder.

technology

Technology deals with the many ways in which we make and build things. It puts science to work for us. Technologists study how we can use different materials to make things. Most things today are made by machines. Machines and engines play a very important part in modern technology.

Every part of technology needs its own skills. Space technology helps us to explore outer space and to travel beyond the Earth. Information technology is finding new and exciting ways for us to communicate with one another.

telecommunications

See **communications**.

telegraph

See **communications**.

telephone

The telephone is our most common way of making long-distance communications. It sends speech along telephone lines. The part you hold in your hand is called the handset. It has a mouthpiece and an earpiece.

The mouthpiece contains a microphone, which changes the sounds of your voice into electrical signals. These signals travel along telephone lines to the person you are calling. They go to a kind of loudspeaker in the person's earpiece, which reproduces the sound of your voice into the listener's ear.
See also **communications**.

Nowadays, you can talk to people on the telephone anywhere in the world.

telescope

A telescope is an instrument for looking at faraway objects. It uses lenses or mirrors to collect light and to produce a bigger, or magnified, picture of the distant object.

teletext

See **videotex**.

television

Television is a way of bringing pictures and sounds from faraway places into our homes. It sends, or transmits, these sounds and pictures by using **radio** waves.

A television camera takes pictures of a scene. Inside the camera, the pattern of light in the pictures is changed into a pattern of electrical signals. These picture signals and sound signals are added to a radio wave and then transmitted. At home, an aerial picks up the radio wave and feeds it to a television set. The television signals are changed into pictures on a screen and sounds from the television's loudspeakers.
See also **cathode-ray tube**, **communications**.

textiles

Textiles are fabrics and other materials made from thin threads, or fibres. Textiles include felt, rugs, carpets and sacks. Natural fibres such as cotton and wool have been used to make textiles for thousands of years. Today, **synthetic fibres** are also widely used.
See also **loom**, **spinning machine**.

TGV

A TGV is a very fast French train. TGV stands for *Train à Grande Vitesse*, which is French for high-speed train.

See also **transport**.

flat mirror

incoming light from stars

curved mirror

eyepiece lens

main lens

The TGV travels on specially laid tracks at speeds of 270 kilometres (km) an hour or more. It is powered by electric motors.

theodolite

See **surveying**.

A telescope that uses lenses to gather light from the stars is called a refractor (left). One that uses mirrors is called a reflector (above).

eyepiece lens

tidal power

Tidal power is produced by using the energy in the tides of seas and oceans. In some parts of the world, the difference between high and low tides can be 10 metres (m) or more. The energy of the water as it flows backwards and forwards with the tides can be used to spin water **turbines**. They turn electricity generators.

▷

A collection of different tools used for hammering, cutting, sawing and gripping.

tool

We use different tools to help us cut and shape materials, and to fasten and mend things. Most of these tools are hand tools, which we hold and move with our hands. Some are powered by electric motors. Factories use powerful tools called machine tools.

Some of the most common hand tools are cutting tools. They include knives, scissors, saws and chisels. Knives and scissors have a straight cutting edge. Saws have a cutting edge made up of sharp teeth. Large scissors are called shears. Chisels have the cutting edge at one end.

Drills cut holes in materials. They work by a turning, or rotary, action. You may need to drill a hole for a screw or bolt. You tighten a screw with a screwdriver, and use a spanner to fasten a nut onto a bolt. Pliers are a useful gripping and cutting tool.

When materials have been shaped roughly to size, they need to be made smooth. Planes are tools for smoothing wood, and files are used to smooth metal. See also **machine tool.**

tractor

A tractor is a vehicle that pulls things. Farm tractors pull equipment such as ploughs. Lorry tractor units pull trailers for transporting goods. Most tractors have a **diesel engine**.

train

A train is a vehicle that travels on the railways. It is made up of a **locomotive** and a number of passenger carriages or goods wagons. The locomotive provides the power to pull the train.

tram

A tram is a passenger vehicle that travels on rails in city streets. It is powered by electricity from overhead wires. A trolley-bus is powered in the same way as a tram. It has wheels like a bus.

transmitter

A transmitter is part of a communications system. It is an electronic device that sends out messages or signals. In a telephone, the transmitter is the microphone inside the mouthpiece. Radio and television transmitters produce radio waves that carry sound and picture signals. These signals are then sent out from tall transmitting aerials.
See also **telephone, television.**

▷

A tram travels along a street in Prague, in the Czech Republic. The frame on top of the tram picks up electricity from overhead cables.

BALABENKA

6884

Transport

Cars, buses, lorries, trains, ships and aeroplanes are our main means of transport by land, sea and air. They carry people, materials and goods from place to place.

Transport by land depends on wheels. The first wheeled wagons, drawn by oxen, came into use about 5500 years ago. Horse-drawn carriages were the main form of transport until the early 1800s. By the late 1800s, people began travelling on roads in 'horseless carriages'. These were powered by **petrol engines**. The age of the motor car had begun.

Transport by sea also began about 5500 years ago. People put to sea in sailing ships that used the power of the wind. Today, most ships are powered by **diesel engines** or steam **turbines**.

Transport by air began in the early 1900s. In 1900, Count von Zeppelin in Germany began building huge airships. The Wright brothers in the United States built and flew the first aeroplane three years later. In the late 1930s, new kinds of aircraft began to appear in the skies. They included the helicopter and the jet.

Planes get ready to depart from London's Gatwick Airport. Almost 23 million passengers pass through the airport every year.

aircraft

Aircraft are vehicles that fly in the air. The most common one is the aeroplane. Other aircraft include the **glider** and the helicopter. All these aircraft are heavier than air. Balloons and airships are lighter than air.

airport

An airport is a place where aircraft take off and land. Tens of millions of passengers pass through international airports across the world every year. At busy airports, aircraft take off and land every few minutes.

Among the many activities that take place at an airport are checking in passengers, handling baggage, refuelling the planes and servicing the engines. In a control tower at or near the airport, air-traffic controllers use **radar** to find the positions of all aircraft on the ground, taking off and coming in to land.

container

A container is a large box that contains different kinds of goods. It can be carried by road, railway or sea. Special handling equipment is used at container terminals to move the containers between lorries, railway wagons and container ships.

▷ *A container ship carries goods in containers that are stacked on its flat deck.*

mass transit

Mass transit is a transport system that can carry large numbers of passengers. It transports them over short distances in a short time. Mass transit systems are used in cities, where the roads often become blocked with traffic. A mass transit system may include buses, trams, an underground railway and a surface railway.

Many cities now have mass transit railways. The tracks run on the surface, underground and above ground level.

railway

A railway is a transport system in which trains run on steel rails. On most railways, the track consists of two rails which are placed exactly 143.5 centimetres (cm) apart. This is called the standard gauge. Tracks with rails which are closer together are known as narrow gauge.

The United States has the world's biggest railway network, with over 350 000 kilometres (km) of track. Britain has about 16 000 km of railway track, on which there are around 2600 stations.

▽ *Railway tracks are made up of steel rails that are welded together in long lengths. The rails are supported by shorter cross-pieces called sleepers.*

◁ *Concorde is the world's fastest airliner. It travels at speeds of up to 2350 kilometres (km) an hour, which is twice the speed of sound.*

port

A port is a place where ships load and unload passengers and cargo. Ports are built in natural or artificial harbours, where the waters are calmer. They have facilities for ships to dock, and equipment such as cranes for lifting cargo. Some ports have dry docks for repairing ships. A dry dock is a basin from which the water can be drained out.

ship

A ship sails on the seas. Most ships are driven by **propellers**. They are powered by **diesel engines** or steam **turbines**. Ships are a slow form of transport. This is because **friction** slows them down. Liners and ferries are ships that carry passengers. Freighters carry cargo. Special kinds of freighters include container ships and oil tankers.

truck

A truck is another name for a lorry.

tunnelling

Tunnelling means digging a hole under the ground. Tunnels are dug, or bored, in mines. They are also used to carry water supplies. The biggest tunnels are bored to carry roads and railways. Many road tunnels have been bored through the Alps in Europe. They were made through the hard rock using explosives.

turbine

A turbine is an engine with wheels that spin round. The wheels are spun round by liquids or gases. Water turbines are used to drive the generators in **hydroelectric power** stations. In other power stations, steam turbines are used to spin the generators. Jet engines contain gas turbines.
See also **jet engine**.

two-stroke engine

Some motorbikes have a two-stroke engine. It produces power once in every two movements, or strokes, of its **pistons**.
See also **motorcycle, petrol engine**.

typesetting

Typesetting is putting together letters and words in lines ready for printing. Today, most letters, or type, are formed by computers that use fine **laser** beams. Less modern typesetting is done by arranging bits of metal that are shaped as individual letters.

typewriter

A typewriter is a small printing machine. It prints words on paper, one letter, or character, at a time. A typist taps a key, for example b, on a keyboard. Levers push a piece of type with a b on it against an inked ribbon and onto the paper.

U

flow of steam

casing

blades

rotor

turbine wheels

Machines like this were used to bore the Channel Tunnel under the English Channel. The front part of the machine rotates and slowly grinds away the rock.

The rotor in a steam turbine spins round when steam rushes through the blades of the turbine wheels.

underground railway

An underground railway travels in tunnels below the surface. It is sometimes called a subway or a metro. Underground railways are useful in busy cities because they are not affected by traffic jams on the streets above. The London Underground (opened in 1863) was the first underground railway and is still the biggest in the world.
See also **transport**.

uranium

Uranium is a kind of metal. It is used as fuel in nuclear power stations. Atoms of uranium can be made to split. When they do, enormous amounts of **nuclear energy** are given out as heat.

valve

A valve controls the flow of a liquid or a gas. A water tap is a kind of valve that you can open and close. Tyres have one-way valves. They let you pump air in, but the valve stops the air from escaping. Valves inside **petrol engines** let fuel and air into the cylinders, and allow burned gases to pass out.

hooks

loops

VDU

VDU is short for video display unit. It is the name for a computer screen. See also **computer.**

Velcro

Velcro is a kind of fastener. It is made of tiny plastic hooks and loops. Velcro is often used instead of a zip fastener to join together pieces of fabric.

vice

A vice is a device for holding something firmly. When you work on a piece of wood with a tool, for example, you place the wood in a vice to hold it steady.

videocassette recorder

A videocassette recorder, or VCR for short, is a machine on which you can record and play back television programmes. You can also play back recorded films. The programmes and films are recorded on a wide **magnetic tape** called a videotape. It is enclosed inside a **cassette.** The machine is also called a videotape recorder, or a video recorder.

videotex

Videotex is the name of the systems that call up information on a television screen. There are two main systems, called teletext and viewdata. They both use information, or data, that is stored in a powerful computer.

In a teletext system, the information is broadcast with television programmes. In the United Kingdom, Ceefax and Oracle are examples of teletext systems. In a viewdata system, the information travels to the television set along telephone lines.

Velcro fasteners are used, for example, in clothing, sports shoes, and cushion and duvet covers.

viewdata

See **videotex.**

virtual reality

Virtual reality is the use of computers to create an imaginary world that appears like the real world. To explore this world, you wear a special helmet with a built-in screen. You see different views on the screen as you turn your head. You can wear a special glove that lets you 'touch' objects in the imaginary world.
See also **simulator.**

VTOL

VTOL is short for vertical take-off and landing. A VTOL aircraft, for example a helicopter, takes off directly upwards.

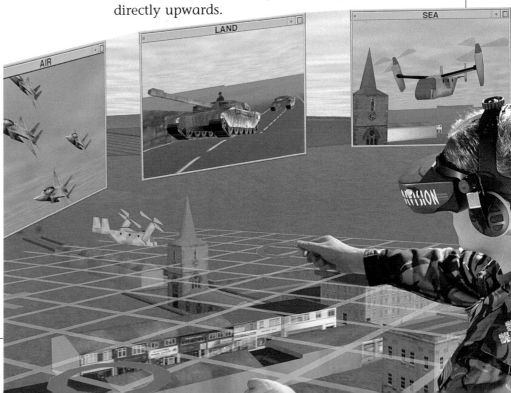

A soldier uses virtual reality to help him work out how to fight battles. By looking in different directions he gets different views of what is happening.

W

waste disposal

Waste disposal means getting rid of waste materials. On average, people in Europe and the United States throw away more than 2 kilograms (kg) of rubbish every day. This rubbish includes cans, paper, cardboard, bottles and plastics.

Some people send waste materials to be recycled. But most waste is put in the dustbin and then taken from our homes. It is either burned or buried in huge pits. Rubbish in pits is known as 'land-fill'. This method of waste disposal is a great waste of materials and land.
See also **recycling, sewage treatment.**

watch

A watch is a small clock that you wear on your wrist. Some watches work mechanically. Their hands are turned by a system of tiny **gear** wheels, which are driven round by a spring. Digital watches have no hands. The time is shown by numbers, or digits. Digital watches are powered by a tiny battery. They are often called quartz watches because they measure time by counting the very quick movements of crystals of quartz. Some quartz watches have hands to show the time.

The insides of a mechanical watch (right). The rocking movement of a balance wheel is used to measure time. This movement lets the gear wheels move slowly, to turn the hands. A digital watch (left) uses a quartz crystal to measure time.

digital display (LCD)

balance wheel

gear wheels

jewel bearings

water closet

A water closet (WC) is another name for a toilet or lavatory. It gets rid of human waste into the sewage system. A stream of water flushes the waste away. It leaves the WC through a bent pipe. Water trapped in the bend stops smells from rising up through the sewage pipes.

water power

See **hydroelectric power, tidal power, wave power.**

water supply

The water supply is the water that comes into our homes, factories, schools and businesses through pipes. The water often starts its journey in a distant river or lake. It is piped first to waterworks, where it is treated so that it is fit to drink. Chemicals such as chlorine are added to the water to kill any germs. The water is then filtered to make it crystal clear. Finally, the water is piped to our homes and to other buildings.

wave power

Wave power is produced by using the energy of the waves in seas and oceans. It is a kind of **alternative energy.** Several ways of using wave energy have been invented. None of them is suitable yet for large-scale use.

weaving

See **loom.**

weightlessness

See **space technology.**

Waves contain a huge amount of power when they rise to be several metres high. They can give surfers an exciting ride.

wheel and axle

See **winch**.

winch

A winch is used to lift heavy loads. It is an example of a simple machine called the wheel and **axle**. A simple hand winch has a drum with a rope wound around it. It is called a windlass. When the handle is turned, the drum turns round and winds up the rope. Cranes use winches that are driven by engines.

Some of the many kinds of wheels used on different vehicles and in various machines.

wind power

Wind power is the use of the energy blowing in the wind. It can be used to generate electricity. The windmill was the first machine to use the wind's energy. Today, windmills have been replaced by wind **turbines.** Most of them have huge **propellers**, which spin round when the wind blows. The propellers turn generators to produce electricity. In places, groups of wind turbines have been built to create wind 'farms'. See also **alternative energy.**

wind tunnel

A wind tunnel is a structure through which air is blown or sucked. Aircraft and vehicle designers use wind tunnels to test new aircraft and vehicles. They can find out how well their designs 'slip' through the air. They try to make their designs as **streamlined** as possible to reduce **air resistance.** Other engineers use wind tunnels to test the effects of the wind on structures such as bridges.

welding

Welding is a very common method of joining pieces of metal. The pieces are held together and then heated strongly where they touch. The metal there melts and mixes. When it cools, it forms a strong joint between the pieces. Extra metal may be added to the joint during welding. Burning gas or electricity may be used to produce the high temperatures that are needed for welding.

Sparks fly as a welder uses an electric welding torch to make a metal joint.

wheel

The wheel is one of the most important inventions ever made. One of its first uses, in about 3500 BC, was as a potter's wheel to make pottery. But people soon discovered how to make wheeled carts, which became the main way of transporting goods. Without the wheel, there would be no cars, bicycles or trains. There would be few machines or engines. Most of them use wheels of some kind, particularly **gear** wheels.

wing

The wings of an aircraft keep it up in the air. They are made in a special shape, which is called an aerofoil. When the wings move through the air, the air pressure above them drops slightly. The air underneath tries to force the wings upwards. When an aeroplane travels fast enough, the lifting force on its wings becomes so strong that the aeroplane lifts off the ground and flies.
See also **aeroplane, hydrofoil**.

wire

Wire is a thin thread of metal. It is made by pulling a metal rod through smaller and smaller holes in special pieces of equipment called **dies**.

wood

See **materials**.

Using a word processor, it is quick and easy to set out and print letters and other documents.

word processing

Word processing means preparing and printing out words by using some kind of computer. A simple word processor is like a typewriter with a small screen. It has a small memory which can store words and sentences that you use regularly.

More powerful word processors have a large memory and a bigger screen. They can store many different instructions for moving and arranging the words that are typed in. Word-processing programs for computers do the same things. For example, they let you alter the text you have typed, move around paragraphs, check the spelling, change the size and style of the type, and so on. You only need to print out the text when you are completely happy with it.

Zip fasteners have been in use for more than 100 years.

X Z

xerox

A xerox is another word for a photocopy. The word comes from xerography, which is the name for the process that most photocopiers use.

Xerox is also the name of one make of photocopier. See also **photocopier**.

X-ray machine

Doctors use an X-ray machine to look inside the human body. An X-ray machine produces invisible waves called X-rays. They are a kind of **radiation**.

When an X-ray is taken, the rays pass through your body and are recorded on a piece of film. They pass easily through your flesh, but not through the bones. The X-ray photograph shows whether any of your bones are broken. X-ray machines are also used at airports to detect dangerous metal objects, such as guns and knives, on passengers or in their luggage.

zip fastener

A zip fastener is a fastening device for clothes. It has two tapes with rows of tiny teeth. The teeth are made of metal or hard plastic. When you do up a zip, a clip joins the teeth so that they lock firmly together.
See also **Velcro**.